# FOLK DANCE

## PHYSICAL EDUCATION ACTIVITIES SERIES

Consulting Editor:
AILEENE LOCKHART
University of Southern California
Los Angeles, California

Evaluation Materials Editor:
JANE A. MOTT
Smith College
Northampton, Massachusetts

ARCHERY, Wayne C. McKinney
BADMINTON, Margaret Varner Bloss
BADMINTON, ADVANCED, Wynn Rogers
BASKETBALL FOR MEN, Glenn Wilkes
BASKETBALL FOR WOMEN, Frances Schaafsma
BIOPHYSICAL VALUES OF MUSCULAR ACTIVITY, E. C. Davis,
    Gene A. Logan, and Wayne C. McKinney
BOWLING, Joan Martin
CANOEING AND SAILING, Linda Vaughn and Richard Stratton
CIRCUIT TRAINING, Robert P. Sorani
CONDITIONING AND BASIC MOVEMENT CONCEPTS, Jane A. Mott
CONTEMPORARY SQUARE DANCE, Patricia A. Phillips
FENCING, Muriel Bower and Torao Mori
FIELD HOCKEY, Anne Delano
FIGURE SKATING, Marion Proctor
FOLK DANCE, Lois Ellfeldt
GOLF, Virginia L. Nance and E. C. Davis
GYMNASTICS FOR MEN, A. Bruce Frederick
GYMNASTICS FOR WOMEN, A. Bruce Frederick
HANDBALL, Michael Yessis
ICE HOCKEY, Don Hayes
JUDO, Daeshik Kim
KARATE AND PERSONAL DEFENSE, Daeshik Kim and Tom Leland
LACROSSE FOR GIRLS AND WOMEN, Anne Delano
MODERN DANCE, Esther E. Pease
RACQUETBALL/PADDLEBALL, Philip E. Allsen and Alan Witbeck
PHYSICAL AND PHYSIOLOGICAL CONDITIONING FOR MEN, Benjamin Ricci
RUGBY, J. Gavin Reid
SKIING, Clayne Jensen and Karl Tucker
SKIN AND SCUBA DIVING, Albert A. Tillman
SOCCER, Richard L. Nelson
SOCCER AND SPEEDBALL FOR WOMEN, Jane A. Mott
SOCIAL DANCE, William F. Pillich
SOFTBALL, Marian E. Kneer and Charles L. McCord
SQUASH RACQUETS, Margaret Varner Bloss and Norman Bramall
SWIMMING, Betty J. Vickers and William J. Vincent
SWIMMING, ADVANCED, James A. Gaughran
TABLE TENNIS, Margaret Varner Bloss and J. R. Harrison
TAP DANCE, Barbara Nash
TENNIS, Joan Johnson and Paul Xanthos
TENNIS, ADVANCED, Chet Murphy
TRACK AND FIELD, Kenneth E. Foreman and Virginia L. Husted
TRAMPOLINING, Jeff T. Hennessy
VOLLEYBALL, Glen H. Egstrom and Frances Schaafsma
WEIGHT TRAINING, Philip J. Rasch
WRESTLING, Arnold Umbach and Warren R. Johnson

PHYSICAL EDUCATION
ACTIVITIES SERIES

# FOLK DANCE

**LOIS ELLFELDT**

*University of Southern California*

WM. C. BROWN COMPANY PUBLISHERS
DUBUQUE, IOWA

Printed in United States of America

# Preface

There is amazing similarity among folk dances, no matter what the land of their origin. Although there are many descriptions of dances available, there has been little clarification of differences in performance that make each dance unique. This book is designed to describe the elements of folk dance, to elucidate some aspects of style, and to show the similarities and the differences of various forms.

Because of the enormous range and diversity of this subject, discussion of styles is limited to some European and Israeli forms of folk dance which are most popular in schools. This book should prove useful not only as a student text but as a guide for teachers and for those participating in community folk dance programs.

Self-evaluation questions are distributed throughout the text to provide the reader with typical examples of the kind of skills and understanding which he should be acquiring. These are, of course, merely representative; the reader should devise additional ones as a self-check on his own progress.

Once the reader has grasped the fundamentals outlined in this introductory text, he will be prepared for more advanced study and for further reading in this fascinating field of dance.

# Contents

# What Is Folk Dance?

Images of peasants in gaily colored costumes, embroidered shirts, and shiny black boots come to mind at the mention of "folk dance." Girls in laced bodices whirl ruffled skirts and toss beribboned braids. Flashing-eyed young men with trim waists and full sleeves jump and stamp. Echoes of plaintive Gypsy melodies, persistent rhythms, and sharp cries ring in our ears. Or the word may jog memories of a childhood experience where little boys in stocking caps pulled little girls in fancy costumes around the school Maypole, wrapping crepe paper streamers about the pole and each other.

Like most stereotypes, these impressions have superficial bases in fact. Folk dancers often wear gaily-colored costumes, most include men and women; and, to the untrained ear, much folk music may be dismissed as "Gypsy music." The idea of children dancing is charming, but the haphazard use of "some little dance they know" and a Maypole device does not necessarily result in the spirit of a celebration for an awakening earth!

To the casual observer, the folk dance spectacle may seem an odd display of creatures moving in exotic ways. But to one with some understanding of people and tradition, their dances enrich understanding not only of differences but of those things which they have in common.

Usually, we associate folk dance with the historical and inevitably traditional behavior of people from foreign lands. Somehow, these dances *were* so associated; and as we watch them, we try to recapture something of a different time and place. But we must understand that, while much dance is traditional, folk dance is also a *living* form of behavior with a character reflecting people and their world. Some of the old will always remain; much that seems new appears. There are fresh emphases, changing qualities, different values. It's the same movement but a different performance. And there is equal value in current interpretations as well as in the "authentic," historical dances of people. Unfortunately, we tend to perceive folk dance as frozen in a traditional and unchanging mold rather than as an expression of contemporary man.

## DEFINITION

Folk dance is an action form resulting from people's selection and organization of human movement; its intangible value appears to be in the actual participation. When it becomes a spectacle to watch, it loses its most characteristic feature—that of people themselves moving. Similar to play, with occasional bursts of competition among the dancers, it is based upon conscious control of energy and rhythm, upon planned design in space and in relationship with others.

In its simplest definition, folk dance means "the dance of the people." But all dance implies people, except for poetic references to dances of raindrops, atoms, or whooping cranes. "People dance" appears to celebrate man's interaction with other men. Organized according to his ideas and needs, it reflect his reassurance as a member of his group. Initially serving as reinforcement for important events in everyday life, folk dance has become a part of evolving custom and history. Among some, it is not "who are you?" but "what do you dance?"

Just as it is difficult to generalize about people, so it is confusing to make general statements about their dance. Both must be considered within the framework of a time and a place. Yet there are common elements among people and their dance forms, regardless of time and place.

The action of folk dance is relatively simple, usually developing out of natural gesture and ways of moving through space. But the action no longer serves its original function and is structured into a formal sequence of movements with spatial design, rhythmic pattern, and implied significance.

## PURPOSE

There are many purposes for these "people participation" dances. Some appear to exaggerate such human motives as work, courtship, or war; some are concerned with religious or political convictions. In many cases they appear to be evidence of man's urge to form movement into patterns of play, action that is just fun to do. But there is more to the genesis of folk dance than mere delight in moving, or even in the personal satisfaction of skilled performance. Even with the most superficial examination, it is clear that there are many purposes.

Whether folk dance is characterized as a semi-superstitious celebration of belief in the magical properties of ritual or as personal gratification in group play or whether it has religious or erotic overtones, it remains a formulation of movement initiated and consumated according to a changing hierarchy of reasons held important by man in his world. Interestingly enough, the dance form itself may change less than the people who dance it, since their reasons for repeating the same dance are not constant.

Today folk dance is considered representative of people of a particular geographic area with common bonds of language, politics, music, and tradition, thus a manifestation of nationalism. While there may be many similarities of pattern and style among folk dances of different countries, especially those with open frontiers, it has come to represent the traditions and festival celebrations allied with a people. Today national dances are performed in costume, on religious or political holidays, or on ceremonial occasions, and then they are put away for another time. No longer is the participation a part of everyday life, but rather it is a symbol of a common heritage.

Unquestionably, there is significance in seeking characteristic movement patterns, points of emphasis and qualities in these surviving dance forms, but an overzealous concern for "the real thing" may result in limiting stereotypes. Current interpretations and popular evidence of "people dance" may add excitement, depth, and significance to the search.

## ORIGINS

Just where or when folk dance began is impossible to say. Earliest man undoubtedly performed movement rituals (perhaps in underground caves where he also painted on the walls) for celebration or survival or maybe as religious ceremony or for socializing around the tribal fire. Communication was very simple then. Stories were told from person to person or from person to group. Some of these must have developed into communal recitation with everyone knowing the characters, plot, sequence of events, and ending. So it was with movement expression, some people performed for others to see, and some for everyone's participation. Even as some stepped out of the group to intercede with unknown powers, so men or women, and sometimes both, participated in the movement rites.

There came to be a time for performance, of showing to others as well as for small and large group participation. Even today, this same kind of differentiation in dance forms exists. The performance types are the Spectacular, the Ethnic, and the Art forms while the participation dances are categorized as Folk Dance, Social Dance, and Dance Therapy.

**3**

# WHAT IS FOLK DANCE?

There is a close relationship between Ethnic and Folk dance; both are concerned with characteristics peculiar to certain groups of people. Ethnic dance is a broad term which identifies a cultural-racial bond, wider in scope than the national character of folk dance. Generally, ethnic dance is performed for others to communicate and celebrate meanings understood by the people concerned. Cultural, religious, and racial heroes, and gods and ideas form its core. For example, in India there are many indigenous folk dances, yet overall there is a rich ethnic form. This content, technique, and style has permeated the Orient, even as the philosophy and religion of India have pervaded these lands. Israel is an example of a country where immigrants have brought folk dances from all parts of the world and these have become a part of Israeli folk dance, but the ethnic dance of the Hebrew is part of his all encompassing religious and cultural custom.

There is an even closer bond between folk and social dance. In truth it is logically impossible to differentiate them. Probably one very tenuous difference is the avowed intent of social dance in contemporary social situations. But current social dance, as well as the older forms, can be considered both social and folk in nature. Certainly, social dance has developed out of the folk forms, changing according to time and place. Current forms, where dancers move opposite but separately, may reflect a new view regarding the equality of the sexes. The more traditional leadership role in the dance position, is however, still highly regarded in some situations.

Many sources of belief and behavior can be found in the records of early man, and so, too, are traces of folk dance beginnings. While there may be overlapping themes for a single dance, one can still identify remnants from earlier forms in the folk dances of today.

MAGIC-RELIGIOUS. The magic-religious source is rich and can be traced to a time before written history. The primitive people danced in order to contact the unknown, to express their needs and fears, and more particularly to seek magical aid for survival. Early dances were performed as the central action of rites, the purposes of which were to gain success in the hunt and security from unknown dangers; to ensure victory; to regain health; and to celebrate important occasions from birth to death such as coming of age, the founding of a home, marriage, laying the ghost of the departed. Apparently there were solemn dances celebrating the conquest of light over darkness, good over evil, power over weakness. And there were lively dances mimicking the animals of the hunt and the sights and sounds of nature. Later these dances, often performed in a circle around a fire or a sacred object, occurred as rites of harvest, sometimes at festivals marking the approach of spring.

Evaluation Questions

Almost all of the dances of today retain traces of these old rites, though their original signifiance has been long forgotten. Certain figures, steps, and patterns are performed as traditional rituals rather than as forms which possess any easily recognizable meaning.

ANIMAL. Animal dances, in which the action of either hunter or hunted is mimed, have persisted to the present day. In many cases the action has been so polished and changed that the animal origin is almost unrecognizable. Such remnants as the turkey-trot, grizzly-bear, bunny-hug, gallop, snake-dance, fox-trot, *pas-de-chat,* and monkey are feeble reminders of these. Transformation is to be expected; as traditional forms are handed down from generation to generation, with differences in purpose, practice, and value, change is inevitable.

WAR. Warlike dances can be traced to the time when man searched for new herds, lands, or triumph in battle with other men. The sound of clashing axes, flashing swords and sticks was, like the primitive bull-roarer, warning to man and beast alike. It has been reported that the same war dance was often performed, not just for war but as a celebration of food or political advantage, simply by changing the rhythm, tempo, or style of performance. This indicates an early adjustment of *way* of performing a dance rather than developing a different sequence of movement figures for a different though related purpose.

AGRICULTURAL. Dance continued to relate to matters of survival, but the patterns of survival were changing. Increased sophistication accompanied new perspectives. Many of the old forms based in mystery and superstition fused into new ways of perpetuating acceptable traditions.

**5**

Which of these formations are found in folk dances of the United States? Can you think of other formations also used in this country?

Evaluation Questions

DANCE FORMATIONS

With the transition to an agricultural economy, the old magic was transferred to planting, harvesting, and the fulfillment of new needs. With the rise of the city-states and a ruling class, dances were developed to celebrate the priestly and noble orders as well as to find relationships with new gods.

With the rise of national states, a new and powerful framework for national life was being built. Now people with common boundaries, of like economy and politics were establishing their own language, tradition, mythology, music, costume, and dance. In spite of a survival of old beliefs and superstitions and with the obvious division of labor and class that was growing, the core of nationalism gave rise to another set of values and characteristics of a people.

OCCUPATIONAL. Dances peculiar to new roles and occupations appeared. There were dances for virgin priestesses in religious temples, and there were dances of weavers who re-enacted the motion of the weaver or the loom. Dances were performed at spring festivals; as prime content for the medieval mystery plays of the church; as a vehicle for rehearsing the elements of chivalry; as part of the splendor, intrigue, and superficiality of the courts of kings. And whatever the occasion, time, or place, peasants frolicked in fields, churchyards, and village squares, half believing the old magic, repeating and decorating the ancient movement patterns.

With changes in specialized work came a refinement of occupational dances. During the Middle Ages, members of the trade guilds were responsible for forming the gestures of their trade into dances. Today there are records of innumerable dances of shoemakers, tailors, coopers, weavers, millers, bakers, farmers, blacksmiths, butchers, and soldiers, to name a few.

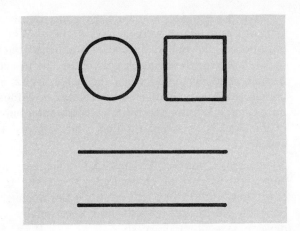

Diagram A:

DANCE FORMATIONS

These work dances so well characterized the occupations represented that they could be easily recognized. Nevertheless, they were usually accompanied by words which further described the action. During the fourteenth and fifteenth centuries, the trade guilds established special days for celebrating these occupations, and one of the features of such occasions was the performance of dances.

SOCIAL. From the earliest times, dance has been a part of special ceremonies dedicated to coming of age, courtship, marriage, and the relationship of man and woman. These themes occur over and over again in the dances of all nations. The fertility rites of the primitives may well have been the forerunner to the many courtship dances which developed into the couple dance in the rural courts of Southern France at the time of the Crusades. At this time the code of behavior basic to our own was initiated. The courtly bow to the lady supplanted a rough embrace; and taking the lady's hand to lead her down the floor took the place of dragging her off by the hair. The lift of the lady in the great fertility leap changed to a restrained turn under the knight's arm. The lady's violent gesture of repulse became a shy turn of the head and a wag of her forefinger.

The polite forms of the courts were transferred to the peasants even as their dances were originally transformed for the elaborately costumed aristocrats of the courts. Members of royal houses throughout Europe set fashions in dance and even made great political alliances as they travelled and danced from country to country.

The legacy of the social dance as an important phase of folk dance was set. Most of the great dances of the courts of France, Italy, Spain, Germany, and England were adapted from the peasants' dances. The

**7**

Gavotte, Allemande, Sarabande, Pavanne, Bouree, Volta, Minuet, Courante, Galliard, and Gigue were a few of these. While they were basic to the evolution of the ballet, they also established the precedent for a surge of social dance for the rising middle class. The pre-classic dances of the courts became suddenly dated when the polka, waltz, and schottische came into popularity. Today in the United States, a Minuet may seem appropriate for a George Washington birthday celebration but it hardly suits the dancers of this age. New styles, rhythms, and patterns develop to fit a new time and need.

TRENDS. Some folk dances have changed little, being repeated again and again as part of an heritage. While the reasons for performing the dance may differ, they still reinforce ties among people. Sometimes, variations of old dances evolve and occasionally comparatively new forms develop in contemporary style.

It is no wonder that it has become increasingly complicated to differentiate among dance forms for there is a great residue of bits and pieces of the old forms, many of which have lost their original reason for being. Also there are the endless variations and reorganizations of pattern and style in terms of practice and use. And none of these will stand still long enough to even be identified accurately.

Folk dances are still danced in some countries; indeed, they are danced in most countries, but for far different reasons than in the beginning. Sometimes they serve an integral role in national or religious festivals. They may occur at harvest or planting time, at weddings, births, deaths, and important social occasions. Because of their vitality, color, and stereotype, they often are used as propaganda, a kind of a living advertisement for the native charms of a country.

In the United States, with people from diverse national origins, remarkably few of these dances have remained popular. In some areas where national origins have been cherished, their language, music, and dance have remained nearly intact. With the acculturation of second and third generations, however, these interests usually change.

Folk dance of the United States is probably identified by many as square dance, derived from the English and French quadrilles; and round dances which use many of the steps of European circle dances. Names given these dances and to the accompanying music are descriptive of typically American characters and events. While the American Indian has folk dances of his own, these scarcely characterize the majority of the citizens of this country.

Square dance forms of American folk dance vary tremendously from Massachusetts to Virginia, Texas to Colorado, Kentucky to California. There are marked differences in tempo, pattern, and style. This divergence evidenced in different parts of a unified country serve only to substantiate the same kinds of differences in Europe, both within a single country and more markedly between different ones.

Participation forms which have been functional to the life of some time and place are often used as the basis for spectacular display forms, almost as a reminder of an earlier time or as a rehearsal of some cherished tradition. Having lost its initial meaning, it now enables some choreographer to choose from its pattern and style a representation of what it was. As a kind of symbol, one pattern replaces another, either in form or in purpose—sometimes in both.

# 2

# Movement Basic to
# Folk Dance

When performing the folk dance of a specific country, the dancer supposedly may learn about the people of its origin. But this is highly questionable, for no matter how often one repeats the mechanics of a dance of some other land, the only thing that becomes quite clear is that each dance employs much the same kind of movement as any other. There is a kind of international commonality in the action of all folk dance.

People assume that the vast range of action comes from some great stockpile of specific movements. In work, play, dance, gymnastics, and acrobatics, indeed in every kind of movement that man does, there seem to be endless kinds of movement, each with its own character. A spectator marvels at the complicated action of a circus acrobat, a premier ballerina, or an Olympic gymnast. But all such complicated movement combinations are based on relatively simple fundamentals which have been rearranged, varied, and affected by changes in dynamics, rhythm, and spatial patterning.

## BASIC MOVEMENT IN ONE PLACE

In one place, without travelling through space, man can flex and extend his joints. He can increase or decrease joint angles, stretch and recoil, push and pull, hit and resist, reach out and gather in, lift and collapse, jump and fall, broaden and narrow, lengthen and shorten. He can rotate, or turn around the axis of a joint by circling, rotating, or rolling, twisting, or pivoting.

The potential complexity of any simple action in one place can be appreciated when one considers that man can move as a single unit or with variations at one or more of his innumerable joints. This might result

**10**

Evaluation Questions

**What do you learn of other countries by learning the steps of their dances?**

in an all-over movement such as: One arm extended to the side, the other pulled up close to the body with wrist and fingers extended; one knee bent and rotated in, the other turned out and extended in a hop from the floor; the head circling to the right and the shoulders twisted to the left; one foot flexed at the ankle and turned in, the other in extension, pushing off the floor. When one realizes the additional possible variation in dynamics, spatial design, rhythmic patterning, relationship to other dancers, and styles of performance, it becomes clear that any simple action can quickly develop into an apparently new and unique one.

## BASIC MOVEMENT THROUGH SPACE

Since locomotion, that is moving from where you are to someplace else, results mainly from action of the legs and feet, there are these two variables to consider. These are basic to any dance form that moves through space, no matter what the land of its origin. Man can move from one foot to the other, resulting in a walk, run, leap, gallop, and slide. While these can be done at different tempos, in different rhythms, and with varying degrees of effort, this is all that can be done from one foot to the other.

Man can also move from one foot to the same foot, and this is always a hop. He can go forward, backward, or to the side, in a curved or straight line; he can crouch low or reach high into the air, but if he is moving from one foot to the same foot, it is still a hop. When man progresses from two feet to two feet or variations including one foot to two feet or two feet to one, he is jumping. Whether he is vaulting over a high bar, reaching for an apple high on a tree, or performing *entrechats*, he is still jumping.

**11**

So man moves in one place by flexing, extending, and rotating any or all of his jointed parts, and often by combining these. He moves through space by going from one foot to another, one foot to the same foot, from two feet to two feet, or by combining these. This is all he can do except to creep, crawl, or walk on his hands, none of which are usual in folk dancing.

## COMBINATIONS OF MOVEMENT IN ONE PLACE AND THROUGH SPACE

Combinations of action both in one place and through space have been performed so many times, and with such apparent ease, that people seem unaware of their components. When man skips, he combines a walking step and a hop. He moves from one foot to the other and then from that foot to the same foot. While irregular in time, with longer on the step than the hop, the skip is a simple combination of a step-hop.

When he gallops, man combines a step with a faster leap, and when he slides he simply steps and keeps his feet in contact with the floor, necessarily leading with one foot. This results in irregular timing, especially as he increases speed.

## TRANSITION ACCORDING TO PURPOSE

The actions just discussed are neither difficult nor unusual for any normal person to perform. Indeed, they are basic to practically everything that man does. The folk dancer uses them at a particular time, in a special place, in relation to other people, and with a very specific use of his energy. No longer does he just walk or turn; it becomes a dance-walk and a dance-turn. The dancer is sensitive to the how, where, when, and why of his movement, and he is able to control it.

And so arises the problem of the movement of folk dance as differentiated from other movements. The important factor is *purpose*. Dancer, athlete, and worker all control their actions to fulfill their purposes.

The tennis player practices the coordination of ball toss with swing of racquet for service and then judges where he must be on the court, and when, to successfully cope with his opponent's return. The action, including swing, lift, reach, twist, hit, fall, pivot, walk, run, turn, reach, swing, hit, turn, and run are all controlled to fulfill his purpose. The rules of the game structure these interactions and clarify his win or loss of point.

The carpenter walks, turns, reaches, pulls, lifts, flexes, extends, hits, and recoils, all to hammer a nail into a board. He does each movement when, where, and how he has judged it to be efficient. He is successful if the board is solid and correctly placed to fit others to come.

So the folk dancer makes similar decisions for controlling his body in moving through the patterns of a formulated dance plan. If the dancer is formulating his own dance, he may improvise, starting and stopping whenever he chooses, but if there is reason to repeat phrases or to be able to recall a sequence, he must consider carefully how he is going and when and where he will arrive.

Long ago, man discovered his capacity for choosing some movements and deleting others. These decisions were apparently an outgrowth of planned design as opposed to randomness, meaningful gesture rather than functional act, implied significance rather than any movement that happened. And folk dance came into being. It seems logical to surmise that some forms survived and became traditional because of popular acceptance and use. It is certain that new folk dances have developed, and as people and conditions change, others will appear.

Traditional folk dances have relatively fixed patterns, and while there are numerous variations and styles of performance, there is usually a set form for some version. Because of the controversial feelings about authenticity, it is often difficult to know what the real form of any dance is. One possible solution to this problem is to question the purpose for doing the dance. Is it just for fun? Is it for socializing, historical record, celebration of a national event, as a vehicle for learning the ritual behavior of people?

## TRADITIONAL FOLK DANCE STEPS

There are many words dedicated to the identification of the action combinations commonly referred to as "tradtional folk dance steps." Each country, of course, uses the symbols of its own language, and the student is faced with the additional task of translating both description and style as well as idiomatic usage. It becomes clear that the movement experience itself as far easier to comprehend than a description of it written in a strange tongue, or indeed in one's own language.

Nevertheless, it is often necessary to depend upon verbal description of dances if the real action is not available for study. It would be impossible to include all of the dance steps originated or used by the people who perform folk dances. The following list represents only those more essential steps, used by all dancers in all lands.

*Balance.* Step on left foot, close right to left and rise on toes, lower heels. 3/4 or 2/4 rhythm.

*Barn dance step.* Run (ct. 1); run (ct. 2); run (ct. 3); hop (ct. 4). Sometimes called a running schottische.

**Can you identify the traditional dance step characterized by this foot pattern?**

Evaluation Questions

A TRADITIONAL STEP

*Bleking step.* 2/4 rhythm. With a low jump, thrust left foot forward with heel on floor (ct. 1); with another jump thrust right foot forward with heel on floor (ct. 2); three successive fast changes, left-right-left (ct. 1-&-2).

*Buzz step.* Step on left foot; bring right to left, bearing weight on ball of right foot while pivoting to the left. Continue, keeping feet close together, pushing with the right foot.

*Closing step.* Non-support foot closes beside support foot and takes weight.

*Cut step.* Standing on left foot, swing right foot forward and leap on right, displacing the left foot.

*Dal step.* 3/4 rhythm. Step forward on left foot, bend knee slightly and prepare for easy low swing forward of right leg (ct. 1); finish swing of right leg (ct. 2); lower left heel and prepare to reverse (ct. 3).

*Hambo.* 3/4 rhythm. Accent 1 and 3 beats. *Man's step:* Bend right knee and stamp forward on left foot (ct. 1); hop and pivot on left foot in clockwise turn (ct. 2); step right, about 12 inches from left (ct. 3). Repeat, always starting left. *Woman's step:* Bend left knee and step backward on right foot (ct. 1); touch left toe in back of right foot (ct. 2); leap forward to left, completing turn with partner (ct. 3).

*Hopsa.* 3/4 rhythm. Leap right (ct. 1); step left behind right foot (ct. 2); step forward right (ct. 3). Turning step also performed in 4/4 and 2/4 rhythm.

*Hungarian break.* Hop on left foot and touch right toe in front of left (ct. 1); hop again on left touching right toe to side (ct. 2); hop on left and close right to left with heel click (ct. 3); hold (ct. 4).

**14**

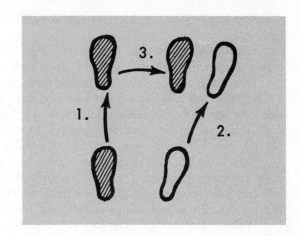

**Diagram B:**

## A TRADITIONAL STEP

*Jig.* Step left to rear of right foot (ct. 1); hop left (ct. &); step right at heel of left foot (ct. 2); hop right (ct. &). This is a simple hop-step, replacing one foot with the other, to the rear.

*Limping step.* An accented walk resulting from a heavier step on one foot than the other.

*Mazurka.* 3/4 rhythm. Glide onto right foot (ct. 1); close left to right with a Cut Step, right foot extending to the right (ct. 2); hop on left foot, bend right knee, pulling right heel close to left ankle (ct. 3).

*Pas de basque.* Leap diagonally forward on left foot (ct. 1); step forward right, in front of left foot and take weight (ct. 2); step back in place on left foot (ct. 3). 3/4 or 2/4 rhythm.

*Polka.* 2/4 rhythm. Hop left (ct. &); step right (ct. 1); close left foot to right (ct. &); step right (ct. 2). The hop has the value of a six-teenth note upbeat resulting in the characteristic polka rhythm. Variations: 1. Hop, run, run. 2. Run, run, skip. 3. Heel, toe, run, run, run.

*Push step.* Step sideward left (ct. 1); bring right foot close to left and change weight (ct. &); push from right foot and step left (ct. 2); bring right foot close to left and change weight (ct. &).

*Schottische.* 4/4 rhythm. Step left (ct. 1); step right (ct. 2); step left (ct. 3); hop left (ct. 4). Variations: 1. Step, close, step, hop. 2. Run, run, run, hop.

*Square dance swing.* Partners in closed dance position with right hip to right hip, feet close together, leaning away from each other, Buzz Step turning clockwise.

*Step-close.* Step in any direction and close with the other foot.

*Step-hop.* Step (ct. 1); hop (ct. & or 2). Step and hop on the same foot.

*Step-swing.* Step and swing free leg. Sometimes, supporting knee bends slightly or heel lifts from the floor with a slight hop.

*Three step turn.* Full turn, taking three steps. Step sideward left (ct. 1); half-turn left pivoting on left foot and stepping sideward right (ct. 2); half-turn left and step sideward left (ct. 3); hold (ct. 4).

*Two-step.* 2/4 rhythm. Step left (ct. 1); close right and change weight (ct. &); step left again again (ct. 2). As a waltz in 3/4 rhythm.

*Varsouvienne.* 3/4 rhythm. Swing left foot past right ankle, toe down, right knee slightly bent (ct. 3 as an upbeat); glide diagonally forward left and take weight (ct. 1); close right to left and take weight, extend left leg (ct. 2); repeat swing of left foot past right ankle (ct. 3).

*Waltz.* 3/4 rhythm. Step left (ct. 1); step right (ct. 2); close left to right and change weight (ct. 3). Variations: 1. Step, close, step (two-step waltz). 2. Run, run, run (running waltz).

# From Words to Movement

A vast literature describes and illustrates folk dances from many lands. These are in the form of pamphlets, syllabi, periodicals, paperbacks, and hard bound editions. Some are difficult to read, some are impossible to translate into action. There are special publications from research groups, folk dance clubs, and federations, as well as from ardent folk dance specialists and eager travellers. Some of these are considered more authentic than others; some are haphazard in description or are poorly edited and ask the reader to perform such impossible feats as "leap onto the left foot and then hop on the right." In spite of such occasional limitations, these materials offer a broad coverage of relatively interesting and reliable description.

Alternatives to the use of such written descriptions of folk dances are the interpretations of other dancers and teachers or an exciting venture into the land of their origin. Certainly, a personal selection and collection of folk dances from the land of their practice would at least satisfy the collector! But don't wait too long. Already, it is hard to find some of the old dances.

It is not easy to learn a dance from verbal description for not only does this involve a different set of symbols, but the descriptions are often long and confusing. They do, however, provide a sound structural and rhythmic form for the dance. It is far easier, however, to learn a dance by having someone tell you what to do or by following dancers who know the pattern.

It is advisable to remember that movement sequences described in words provide only the mechanics. It is like reading a road map and finally arriving at the destination. Trip and destination are uninteresting and bare if the "traveller" misses the scenery and lore of where he has been. The student of the dance needs more than the bare bones of rhythm, space pattern, and step; here he is faced with the crux of the problem. There are plenty of sources describing the mechanics of the dance, but few which clarify the human, intangible aspects of style which determine the real spirit of the dance. Objective analysis of steps, rhythm, design, relationships among dancers, and the formulation into a movement pattern with accompanying music is an important start.

## ANALYZING AND INTERPRETING WRITTEN DANCE INSTRUCTIONS

LEARN THE STEPS. Try to be patient and understand the steps *before* you try to perform the dance. Read over the description and, if necessary, refer to the glossary of folk dance steps provided in most books. Count each movement phrase and relate to the time signature of the suggested accompaniment.

DETERMINE THE RHYTHM. If there is a recommended record or piano score, listen to the music and try to discover the phrases and number of measures for each part of the dance. Be sure that it fits. Sometimes the arrangement of a sequence or number of repeats of a dance will need to be adjusted to fit the music.

When the action occurs is very important, and its relationship to the music should not be overlooked. Following are some aspects of time relationships important to folk dance.

*Rhythm* is the recurrent pattern, sometimes complicated in both movement and accompaniment, especially in dances influenced by complex language patterns or Middle Eastern rhythms.

*Measures* are units of time, usually consistent throughout both dance and accompaniment. In the music it is shown as marked bar lines and recognizable because of the accent.

*Underlying beats* maintain the constant and continual pulse basic to the overall rhythmic structure. For example, the underlying beat of a 4/4 meter is 1-2-3-4, 1-2-3-4, regardless of any superimposed pattern.

*Time signatures* are the numerical symbols placed at the beginning of written music to denote the units of time that make up its rhythm. The number on top indicates how many counts to the measure; the number on the bottom shows the kind of a note that receives one beat. Most common in folk dance are: 4/4, 2/4, 3/4, 6/8, 7/8.

*Phrases* are units of sound or movement which result in a feeling of balance or completion in themselves. In most folk dances, these phrases consist of two, four, or eight measures, similar to folk songs which were adapted to the breath rhythm of singers.

*Tempo* is the rate of speed. Once a tempo has been established, any other speed is either faster or slower.

*Accent* results from a stress, or its absence, which makes it possible to identify patterning by showing contrast. Man's persistent experience with the action of two hands and two feet may explain his easier response to duple meters, where accents fall every two or four beats.

*Upbeat* is the term to indicate a preliminary note or movement before the first action or note of a measure. This is a preparation to "go."

*Musical notation* is the means of recording the rhythmic and tonal relationships of the music. Figure 1 illustrates the rhythmic relationships among simple notes and rests. Figure 2 shows counts for these relationships.

Tonal relationships are indicated by the relative placement of these notes on a five-lined and four-spaced staff. Notes placed above or below this staff are simply extensions of the same staff. Any elementary music

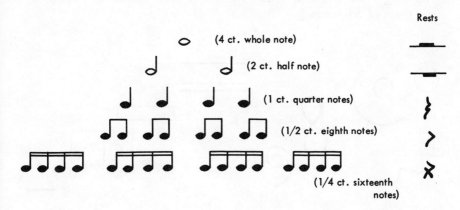

*Figure 1*

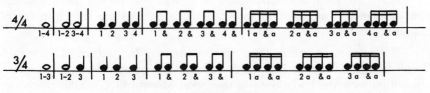

*Figure 2*

book will clarify the melodic form that this takes. While the melodic line is helpful for reproducing a folk dance, the rhythmic pattern is even more important.

UNDERSTAND THE FORMATION. Read the dance description again carefully, and note the formation, direction, and design of each movement sequence. Some folk dances are for one (solo) or two people (couple); some are for four, six, or more. Dances for three individuals are numerous; sometimes these are for one woman and two men or for one man and two women. Other descriptions call for two people as an independent couple or as one of several couples within a group formation. The dance may be progressive, as in a mixer, where man, woman, or both move on to a new partner or couple.

Folk dancers move in a variety of space patterns. Among the more common curved-line formations are the open and closed circles, single curved lines, serpentines, figure-eights, and spirals. (See Figure 3.)

Straight line formations include single-line, double-line (longways), rectangular, square, or triangular shapes. (See Figure 4.) Since all spatial elements are relative, it is vital to establish some "front" or "north" as a fixed point of reference.

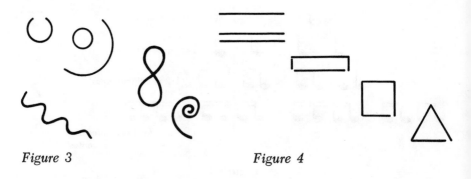

Figure 3                    Figure 4

There are endless combinations of straight- or curved-line formations and even more using both. Some of these formations are shown in figures 5 and 6.

The movement within these formations may be performed at varying *levels* from the floor, as high as the dancer can go with leaps or jumps, to a position with the body close to the floor. Movement can take place over a large or small *range* of space, from a broad to small coverage.

**20**

Determine Relationships with Other Dancers. Try to fit all parts of the dance together, first for one person, then for a partner or other dancers. While the actual steps of most folk dances are relatively simple, there are many ways of holding one's partner or of relating to other dancers. And moving with them is often quite complicated. Some of the more basic positions are:

*Arming.* Partners link left or right elbows.

*Back hold.* Partners face in opposite directions with right sides together, linking right elbows. Girl's left arm crosses behind her back, man reaches for girl's hand behind her back with his right; man's left arm crosses behind his back, girl reaches for man's hand behind his back with her right.

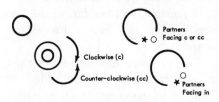

*Figure 5*

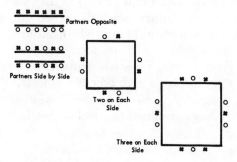

*Figure 6*

*Basket-grasp hold* (for four dancers). Two men stand opposite each other holding their own left wrists with their right hands. With their left hands, they grasp the right wrists of the opposite men. The two women thread their hands under and over the men's hands.

*Closed position* (ballroom). Partners face each other, man holds woman's right hand in his left, man's right arm around the woman's waist, woman's left hand on man's right shoulder, elbow bent.

**21**

*Cross-back hold.* Partners side by side, man at left of woman, hands joined at back, right with right, left with left. Man's right arm is on top.

*Cross hold.* Partners face each other; man holds woman's right hand in his right, left in his left.

*Double-ring grasp.* Alternate men and women. Each man places his his right hand in front of woman on his right, grasping the left hand of the next man; his left hand is in front of the woman on his left in order to grasp the right hand of the next man on his left. Women do the same, joining hands above the men's.

*Hungarian turn position.* Partners face opposite directions, side by side, feet close. Inside hands on partner's outside hip, outside hands held overhead in a curve. As partners turn, they lean away from each other. Sometimes this is taken in a shoulder-waist position.

*Inside hands joined position.* Either facing the same way or in opposite directions, partners grasp inside hands. From here, arms may easily be raised to form an arch.

*One-hand mill.* Four or more dancers grasp right wrist or hand of dancer in front, thumbs on top, arms outstretched.

*Open position.* Facing in the same direction, partners are side by side with the man on the left. Man's right arm is around the woman's waist, woman's left hand on the man's shoulder. Sometimes free hands are joined; sometimes the free hands are on hips or held to the side or overhead.

*Promenade position.* Partners are side by side, facing in the same direction, man on left of woman. Man's right hand grasps woman's right, left hand to left. Man's right hand is on top.

*Reel grasp.* When moving clockwise, partners face each other holding left hands across, right hands on each other's shoulders.

*Scandinavian waltz grasp.* Same as closed position except man's left and woman's right elbows are lifted to shoulder height, and straight.

*Shoulder-waist position.* Partners face each other, man's hands on woman's hips, woman's hands on man's shoulders.

*Square-dance swing position.* Partners are in closed dance position but each is slightly to the left so that right hip is to right hip and inside feet are close.

*Varsouvienne position.* Partners face in the same direction, man to left and slightly behind woman. Man holds woman's left hand in his left, at shoulder height; man's right arm is back of woman holding her raised right hand in his right.

Fit Steps to Rhythm and Space Design. Step and count each part of the dance, slowly. Check constantly with the directions, verifying the rhythmic structure of each step, phrase, and figure. Be sure to count the underlying beat in accord with the time signature of the accompaniment. For example:

3/4  *1*  2  3;  *1*  2  3;  *1*  2  3.
4/4  *1*  2  3  4;  *1*  2  3  4;  *1*  2  3  4.
6/8  *1*  2  3  4  5  6;  *1*  2  3  4  5  6;  *1*  2  3  4  5  6.

Examine each transition from one figure to another, making sure that the step pattern, the count, and the sequence all fit with the underlying beat. Fit all sections of the dance together slowly. Try to proceed through the entire dance without pause. Gradually increase the speed to the pace that suits performance.

SEEK DYNAMICS OF THE ACTION. Try to identify the degree of force necessary for the action. You seldom find any written directions which will help in determining either dynamics or style. Study of any background material about either the dance or the traits of a people, their characteristic gestures, songs, festive occasions, shoes, and costume will be helpful. In most cases, the teacher will have researched whatever possible about the dance, why it is performed, how the accompaniment is played, and how to interpret its purpose and spirit.

*Dynamics* refers to the amount of force used to produce a movement. Greater or lesser force expended in performance is called *intensity*. There are some quite vigorous folk dances and others that seem almost fragile. In some, the dancers seem to glide effortlessly across the floor as if propelled on wheels; and in others, the leaps, stamps, hand claps, and heel thumps are as staccato as drum beats. Any particular stress is called an *accent.*

All aspects of the use of force are important in differentiating style in folk dance. The direction and amount of force produces a number of different *qualities*. There are smooth and unaccented movements, precise bits of sharply accented action, lyrical swings, and moments of suspension as the dancers seem to be hanging in space.

SEARCH FOR CLUES TO STYLE. Investigate available material that is even remotely concerned with the dance. Descriptions of the people, occasion for the dance, folklore, costume and folk music, or anything about the life, traditions, and nature of the people may help in understanding the style of performance. Photographs and motion pictures are an additional aid. If possible, talk with people who have visited the country concerned, particularly those who know the specific dance.

Any library has a central card file which contains references to all available books. Check this file for: Folk Dance; National Dance; Ethnic

**What is the relationship of dynamics of movement to the resulting style of folk dance performance?**

Evaluation Questions

Dance; Poland, Yugoslavia, Greece, or the country in which you are interested; Pageants and Festivals; Folk Music; Folk Tales; Folk Legends; Folk Crafts.

Look in a city or county directory for Folk or Ethnic Group Centers, for recreation or church affiliations relevant to the group concerned. Check with local YWCA, YMCA, YMHA organizations, recreation departments, community centers, colleges, and junior colleges. Scan the local or near newspapers for notices of national group affairs, festival occasions, folk dance clubs, national celebrations, weddings, or religious holidays. Be alert to some of the travel programs on TV, many of which show remarkably good dance sequences. Obviously, there is never time enough to actually learn the dance, but something of the style may be observed.

More and more, there are folk-dance performance groups being seen. Though some of these are quite theatrical, they still retain the essential character of national style. And look into folk festivals that occur in some areas.

The sequential structure and shape of the dance constitute its mechanics; it will come to life only as it acquires a style, a projection of its purpose. In order to better approximate this, it is necessary to learn as much as you can of the people who cherish it.

The best way to learn any folk dance is to go to the land of its origin and to participate in the dance with the people to whom this dance is meaningful. The second best is to be taught the dance by someone sensitive to its styling. By far the most difficult, though the most readily available source, is the written description of the dance.

**24**

# 4

# The Dilemma of Style

From one view, folk dance is an assemblage of steps and patterns of movement in time and space, but from a wider perspective it seems a symbolic formulation of people moving according to their heritage and common nature. The former is easy enough to determine, but the latter is intangible and not only is difficult to identify but is impossible to apply externally to any movement pattern. The real spirit and flavor lies not in the steps and patterns of the dancers but in their manner, style, and conviction in moving.

It is interesting to observe the complicated movement combinations made up by children. One sees fast runs, several tiny hops, a big jump followed by slow walking steps, and then a series of whirling leaps. These movements may be compared to letters in the alphabet which develop into a vocabulary capable of showing relationships in both speech and movement. The child-like action is usually random, reflecting the nature of children free from preconceived structure. Some of these movements are repeated and patterned. Folk dance probably started in much the same way but acquired the traditional and characteristic patterns and styles unique to those who danced it.

## THE MATTER OF AUTHENTICITY

Some descriptions of folk dances are reported as "authentic," others make no such claims. Just what are authentic dances? Are these truly representative of the country? Are they the most popular, the ones most often seen? Are these the ones usually reported? Just what is *authentic* is hard to assess. The very nature of folk materials resists categorization. Even within one area of a country, there are several ways to sing one song,

**What is meant by form in folk dance?**

Evaluation Questions

to dance one dance. And then there is the matter of *when*. It seems that what was performed at one time is not always the same in subsequent performances. Perhaps the simplest solution is to examine a concept of authenticity which is meaningful to you and then refer to the time period concerned and the specific place where this occurred.

In what ways might a person be interested in authenticity? In adherance to some formula? That most people dance this way? That most collectors have reported these?

No, folk dances rarely fit a formula. The only generality that can be made is that a dance has a beginning, a development, and a close. But there are dances consisting of only one step repeated hour after hour, with no apparent beginning or ending—just continuity. Finally, after the dance seemed to have been going on forever, the participants sank exhausted to the ground, but the dance seemed to still go on! Perhaps the sense of a dance stems from the involvement of the people who dance; both are variable. But when a dance has been recorded as a representative dance *done* by a people, there is a very clear beginning, development, and ending; indeed, there is a *way* to do this dance.

If one would count the number of people who perform a dance in a particular way, he would arrive at a questionable average. Then, where did these people learn the dance? Who was the teacher? Is any more known than before about the unique nature of this dance?

## THE SHAPE OF MOVEMENT

Each folk dance, as most people experience it, has its own sequence of movement events, its own rhythmic structure, its own dynamic form.

Evaluation Questions

Can you outline the shape of a
folk dance you have learned?

It is in these variables that the more obvious differences among folk dances
are found.

Any movement that man chooses to perform, and wishes to repeat,
has a sequence and shape which gives it form. The pattern is recognizable
because of the elements which make up its sequence. Some movement
precedes another, and is often repeated. Accents occur and serve as clues
for identification. Some simple and characteristic sequences from folk
dances may be illustrated by: a series of sweeping polka steps followed
by three fast stamps; three sedate schottische steps and four brisk step-
hops; twelve fast, running steps and three staccato jumps.

Whether the dance follows the form of the music or the music follows
the form of the dance is not easy to say. There is no doubt that today the
dancer relies first on the musical form which has been notated and preserved as the music of folk dance.

The matter of how a dance survives to be performed by others is
partially answered by considering the problem of recording movement.
Even today, there is limited use of any system of movement notation,
though *Labanotation* is equally as efficient as musical notation for indi-
cating both simple and complex action with its dynamic, rhythmic and
spatial relationships. There has been almost complete reliance on verbal
description, kinetic memory, or mimetic action for perpetuating the dance.
There is an increasing number of motion picture records of dances, but
it is not easy to learn a dance from watching it on film.

With verbal directions, it is possible to know where you are going,
what steps to use, and when to get there, but little else. *Afficianados* have
devised clever symbols, short cuts, and signals to indicate action, but these

**27**

too are sketchy and difficult to translate into action. Most folk dancers have had the experience of learning a dance "out of a book," and later participating in a dance of the same name with a group of dancers native to the land of its origin. While some steps were familiar, the dynamics, the spirit, and the style made it seem like an entirely new experience. This is the magic of dancers to whom this form has greater significance than the mere skill of performing steps. It is part of their idiomatic gesture, their homeland, their language, legend, and tradition—their unique character as a national group. Perhaps no outsider can ever quite find this real style, for it is something not sought out; rather, it is the result of something you are. Certainly, an attempt to both understand and recapture something of this style can only increase the significance of the dance for you. While it may please the dancer to wear the costume of the country, and surely costume affects the dance, style itself cannot be acquired through the wearing of the most elaborate or authentic costume.

## INTANGIBLE DIFFERENCES

While folk dances have the bond of common means of locomotion, there are subtle differences in the dynamics of the performance. There are certainly no North European walks, Middle Eastern jumps, nor Latin American hops, but there are characteristic ways of doing them. There is a Middle European style, even as there is a German, indeed, even a South German, way of doing a dance walk. It is in this way of performing that the more important differences among folk dances are found. Even with title, musical accompaniment, costume, and appropriate occasion, it is difficult to recapture the differences. It takes an expert, one who has observed and rehearsed the quality, range, patterning, and style to distinguish between a Bavarian and a Brazilian schottische.

A person learns little of a country or its people by simply repeating sequences of movement, but learning the *way* it is performed and the reasons for the dance provides insight. If the student can recapture something of the spirit of the dancers, of the quality and essential nature, he may understand *why* these dances have been cherished and perpetuated. He will certainly know more about the people who dance them.

## STEREOTYPES

There is temptation to become entrapped by readily accesible cliches. It is easy to accept the superficial assumption that all dances from Northern lands are fast, brisk, and jolly while dances of the Latin countries are slow, melancholy, and lyrical. Some examples of these highly questionable stereotypes are:

Primitive dances in which natives whoop it up around an imaginary campfire, with dancers carrying unseen offerings to unknown gods.

Egyptian dances performed in two-dimensional profile; arms wriggling like snakes, hands jutting out at flat angles.

Chinese dancers shuffling about with hands hidden in sleeves or with forefingers jabbing up toward the sky.

Dutch dancers stamping about in wooden shoes or twirling like windmills.

Seventeenth-century minuets by dancers wearing wigs of cotton batting piled high on their heads, mincing about prettily, balancing and bowing to their partners.

Russian dancers in deep knee-bends, kicking out alternate legs, yelling fiercely.

Erect ladies wrapped in Spanish shawls, tapping and stamping their feet haphazardly, clapping their hands in a side-show version of *Flamenco* style.

The use of superficial tricks to identify national characteristics is shoddy and questionable in taste and value. Surely such a substantial form of human behavior deserves more consideration.

## FINDING CHARACTERISTIC STYLE

It is only when one begins to comprehend the importance of the dance form to the people involved that the need for greater understanding is recognized. This is easier to say than it is to do. Finally, it becomes a matter of interpreting what information and experience you have.

There is endless information about many aspects of the nature of people, both historic and geographic. There are written descriptions, histories, legends, conjectures, and documented references; there are photographs, slides, and motion pictures. There are national groups performing at weddings and on national holidays; there are folk festivals and occasional performance groups; there are institutes, clinics, and dance camps. In spite of these potentials for greater insight into style, there is a tendency to depend on almost any substitute for investigating available information.

Almost all folk dance has a multitude of variation. With influences of change as well as the inclination of many to delete some action and to add some new, it is almost impossible to establish any code of performance and still keep the dynamic nature of the form. All of the forces which create variation in a people are at work. Migration of groups, invasion of lands, political uprisings, church edicts, changing values and traditions, available leadership, and propaganda all influence style of performance.

Alternatives for solving the problem seem to be:

1. To assume that the best approximation of style will be found by broad reading, by participation in the dance, and by observation of the people

Can you account for the stereotypes which have developed about
folk dance?

Evaluation Questions

and dance of a specific area. This presumes that one example is representative of the rest of the country, both past and present.
2. To attempt to find materials relevant to changing times and places. While this is quite possible in terms of historical facts, it is likely to be sketchy in relation to folk dance.

In any case, the results will always be formulated in interpretation. With the most reliable data, the best approximation of authenticity will be found. Certainly either of these approaches will be more satisfying than merely duplicating the mechanics of the movement and, as an afterthought, adding superficial stereotypes of style.

# 5

# Clues to Style

Following are generalized approximations of style which can do little more than direct the reader's attention to some aspects of movement according to geographic location. They are designed to be read in conjunction with a dance expression of the country or can be read for the sake of comparison. While there are countless variations of any dance, the variations have many elements in common. The same combinations of movement, however, seem different because of their quality, accent, and style. Obviously, none of these differences occur abruptly at any geographic frontier, because the interaction of many unidentified forces has resulted in a confusing blur of preferences. While different ways of performing the dance are easy to observe, they are difficult to identify in words. More meaningful interpretations can be made after comprehensive examination of direct references to the time and place concerned.

## ALPINE REGIONS OF AUSTRIA, BAVARIA, AND SWITZERLAND (CELTIC-TEUTONIC)

Basic dance steps of this area include the waltz, the two-step, the schottische, and the polka, each of which is usually performed in simple and direct pattern, rhythm, and accent. There are many turns, both individual and around partners. Most of the dances are performed with partners in circles, chains, or processionals. Dance songs are rare but yodels often accompany the dances.

While the Swiss dances are usually sedate and well controlled, the Austrian and Bavarian forms are lively and noisy. There are deep swings and lifts of the entire body, especially in the turning dances. The men stamp and then soar off with an upward lift. The women turn under their partner's arms and then around their partners. Often they spin so rapidly that their full skirts billow out into a great bell.

The men sometimes swing the girls high in the ancient fertility leap. They snap their fingers; slap thighs, buttocks, heels, knees, and cheeks; they clap hands and shout in complicated rhythms even as they hop, jump, or leap around their spinning partners.

In some of the courtship couple dances, the men thrust their thumbs under their suspenders and flap their elbows like crowing cocks. The men hold their partners by hands or around waists with the other hand just back of the hip.

## BASQUE REGIONS OF NORTHERN SPAIN
## AND SOUTHERN FRANCE

It is generally agreed that the most ancient European language, music, and dance comes from these people of unknown origins. Their folk dances are almost always performed by the men, with only a few sedate and lyrical dances performed by women. The men perform great leaping steps with a twisting of the body in the air that is characteristic of many other mountain people. There is great skill and precision in these dances as well as spontaneity and fire in their performance.

The dances are usually in irregular and often mixed rhythms of 5/4, 5/8, or 7/4 meter. Accompaniment is usually sung, the women in high, clear voices and the men in low, heavy tones. Some of the steps of ballet must have been adapted from these dances for *entrechats, grands battements, jettes-battus, pas de basques,* and *ronds des jambes* are found in many dances.

There are processionals, fertility ceremonies, animal dances, Maypole dances, and a wide range of sword dances in which men perform intricate figures while the women beat the rhythm and sing the accompaniment. In one of the *mascardas,* elaborately costumed and masked men leap and hop around a wine glass. Whatever the dance, the men emphasize strength, agility, and skill in interacting with other dancers in extremely complicated patterns. The women always move quietly, with smooth, flowing action, their gaze demure and directed toward the earth.

## BULGARIA (SLAVIC)

From a confusing pattern of migration, resettlement, and intermarriage, the Bulgars seem to have absorbed many of the ancient Slav ceremonies of the land they invaded. In spite of Turkish domination, many of the old *Horos* (chains) have been kept intact, especially in the more remote mountain regions.

In most of the circle dances, the bodies are held solemnly erect and tense. The sequence is simple with some embellishment of the basic step; in some of the couple dances, which develop into large group dances, the men exhibit great imagination and skill. Displays of virility by men and tests of endurance for women are found in many dances. The woman's fast run alternating with a rocking action on the toes, taken in a 2-2-3 pattern, is characteristic. Some of the *Horos* move in a phrase of 5 or 7 eighth or sixteenth notes which may result from Turkish influence.

The following action, moving clockwise in a circle, is an example: Step on right foot, in front of left (ct. 1-2); step on left foot, just behind right (ct. 3). This is usually repeated three or four times. Step side on right foot (ct. 1); hop on right foot and swing left (ct. 2-3); step side left (ct. 1); hop on left and swing right (ct. 2-3).

In Bulgaria, as in Roumania and Yugoslavia, there are three distinct kinds of *Horos*. In the closed circles of the Northern plains, a shaking action occurs; on the mountain slopes, the circle opens and the progression takes place with hops; in the Black mountain areas, the open circle dance is done with trembling and pulsations of the dancers.

## CZECHOSLOVAKIA (SLAVIC)

Czechoslovakia has a diverse population of Moravians, Slovakians, and Bohemians with influences from the Austro-Hungarians, Germans, and Gypsies. The dances have mixed rhythms, often very complex, to fit the words of accompanying songs. While most of the dances are similar to those of other Slav countries in rhythmic and emotional contrasts, these have marked dynamic changes in both song and dance. In one circle dance (*Do Kola*), there is a slow and solemn procession, with feet close to the floor, followed by rapid turns lifting off the floor from the ball of the foot. In another (*Kalamajka*), a sharp hopping step contrasts with a smooth, unaccented run. A lyrical section alternates with gay and lively jumps and stamps. The heels click and the dancers soar into the air.

In most of the progression steps, the feet are placed flat on the floor only to rise onto the toes for turns. There seems to be an extra bounce as the dancer slides or steps and then rises onto the toe. In the circle dances of the Eastern part of the country, arms swing and dancers turn under kerchiefs, and they mime the actions of work. It is only in the West that the couple dance is popular, and here there are waltzes, polkas, and many turning and fast forms. Line dances are performed throughout the country.

The wheeling *Kolos* usually start slowly, with a wave-like rise and fall of the dancers. The vocal accompaniment accents the heavy and solid underlying beat. With the repeat, the entire action speeds up, to return again to the slow processional-like beginning.

## ENGLAND (CELTIC)

The *Morris Dance* is probably the oldest dance performed today in England. Similar to some of the Basque dances, it reflects a Moorish origin. In a circle, square, or longways set, the dancers move in and out of formation, each taking a turn and then returning to place. The equality of performance is characteristic. The dancers are poised with their bodies inclined in the direction of their action. Their arms swing loosely and their bodies are held erect. So controlled are their movements that they seem to glide over the ground with no unexpected accents. The dancers wear bells and ribbons at the knees, and carry feathers, garlands, swords, sticks, or handkerchiefs in their hands.

*Country dances,* especially those associated with May Games, are part of the English tradition. *Sword dances,* with fast running steps or intricate clogs, are performed in complex figures around and over crossed swords. Here too the patterns are evenly balanced, with each dancer taking his turn. In the dances where leaps occur, they are evenly interspersed to avoid irregular accents.

The action of most of the dances is easy, with precise, neat footwork and an evenly balanced body. The progress is smooth and gliding. Floor patterns, as well as rhythms, emphasize proportion and evenness. With simple steps and interweaving of dancers, mathematically precise designs are formed. There is considerable foot tapping and clockwise circling, as opposed to the counter-clockwise circlings of the Slavs. There is little arm action, and sometimes, when clogs are worn, the beat of the feet is tripled or doubled.

## FINLAND (FINNO-UGRIAN)

There are many dance songs of Finland, especially from legends and poetry of nature, like the *Kalevala.* While there is much of the old poetic form, there is virtually nothing left of the old movement forms. Most of the older dances started with a marked upbeat, but newer ones start firmly on the first accent and maintain a regular rhythm throughout. As in some Finnish music where a single note or phrase is repeated, in some of the folk dances there is a kind of follow-the-leader action where steps of preceeding dancers are repeated over and over. These may be the circling runs, little jumps, or continuous toe tappings.

A rather strange emotional and rhythmic tension is noted in the dancers, quite unlike other Scandinavian dancers. The patterns of movement, however, are quite similar to those of Sweden. Many prevailing folk dances of today are performed at wedding celebrations, similar to those of many other countries but with a distinct trace of Slavic and Eastern influence.

## FRANCE (CELTIC)

Little remains of the old French folk dance except as it was polished and adapted by the aristocratic courts of the seventeenth and eighteenth centuries. Here the old folk forms were the basis of a courtly spectacle, of which there is an excess of information. The sources of these dances represent the real folk dance of France which is rarely performed today.

The *Bouree,* a rustic clog dance of Central France, was a courtship dance in which the man, stamping, clapping, and shouting, performed for his lady who was alternately shy and bold. The *Farandole,* from Southern France where the troubadours originated the court dances, was a rollicking chain for men and women following a leader, connected to each other wtih handkerchiefs. The *Branle,* an extension of the *Farandole,* was a slow, simple dance with a leader. The steps consisted of a repeated side-close with intermittent knee bends. The *Gavotte,* from the province of Gap, high in the Alps, was a lively courtship dance done in a chain. In Brittany, it is still performed in a rising and falling combination of two-steps, hops, and leg circlings.

In the mountain regions, as in Brittany, there are leaping, hopping, and jumping *Gavottes* still performed today. Men often finish a phrase with the high fertility leap, lifting the woman high into the air. Both Brittany and the mountain regions have serpentine and chain dances like those of Greece and Yugoslavia.

Characteristic old steps still occur: repeated foot tappings, claps and stamps, sometimes alternating with heel-toe touchings; in chain formation, a continual step-close to the side, with knees bending like a little bow as contrast; the twisting of one foot either in front or behind the supporting leg; a rapid tapping of the wooden clog as the foot passes from front to back; a swing forward and back of the arms. The partners are often linked by little fingers or thumbs. Generally the dancers keep close to each other and take small, restrained steps in accord with the underlying beats of the accompaniment.

## GERMANY (TEUTONIC)

Old German Ring Dances or *Caroles* consisted of the gliding low-dances (*basse* dance) of winter and the leaping, hopping, and jumping high-dances (*haute* dance) of spring. All dances had a heavy accent down, and the low-dance glide was taken with a marked knee bend.

Dances today are usually solid, sedate, and uncomplicated rhythmically, with the same number of steps as there are beats to a measure of accompaniment. This results in an even, regular pattern. While there are marked accents, there is little emotional expression.

The two-step waltz, heavily accented on the first beat, and often done in a very fast tempo, is performed by dancers whirling across the floor. The arms are usually wrapped around the partner, and cheek to cheek, in remarkably close contact for such vigorous action. The turning waltz, the sentimental *Allemande* which was adapted for the courts, and Seven Steps (*Siebenspring*) are all popular dances.

In the present state of Luxembourg, the Pilgrim Step was developed. Performed as a religious processional, it was believed to have therapeutic value. There are three steps forward and one backward, or five steps forward and two back. Every time the direction changed, the whole procession would stop and, with knees raised high, would stamp their feet into the earth.

## GREEK (HELLENIC)

Until recent times, men and women danced separately in Greece, though the old chain dances were always led and closed by a man. The few couple dances were not introduced until the time of the Crusades.

There is a close link between the rhythm of the movement and that of accompanying songs. Slow and fast steps match the syllables and words which result in complicated and irregular metric patterns with units of 5, 7, and 9 predominating.

The women's dances are simple and dignified, the men's accented by unusual demonstrations of strength and agility. Most of the dances are performed in open circles thereby precluding individual arm movements except for the leader who waves the inevitable kerchief. The dancers maintain the circle by holding hands, wrists, shoulders, or kerchiefs. The body is held erect and, in the progression step, moves directly over the advancing foot. Because the feet stay close to the ground, there is a smooth and subtle action. Hopping steps are done with a slide by the women, and with a marked upward lift by the men. A chief characteristic of the Greek dance is the continual directional change and facing of the dancer even while he is progressing in any one of these. The leader will often pass his position to another man when he tires or breaks into the center of the circle to perform his own variations.

## HOLLAND (TEUTONIC)

Folk dance of Holland appears to have been adapted from that of many other countries and, with few exceptions, exhibits little that is unique. There is considerable reference to *plugge-dansen,* which is variously described as "a lively couple dance" or "a kind of a *Fandango,*" neither of which illuminate anything of its nature. *Matelot,* a hornpipe, is similar to the English dance and is performed popularly by sailors in heavy wooden clogs. In this, there is considerable bumping, slapping, clomping, pinching, and clowning.

In general the simple group dances are limited to skips, shuffles, walks, waltzes, polkas, and hornpipes. The movement is always close to the floor, rarely lifting to the ball of the foot. The movements have regular accents and inevitably end with a slight body roll and a stamp.

## HUNGARIAN (FINNO-UGRIAN)

Folk dance of Hungary is marked by extremes of melancholy and gaity, fierce pride and tender simplicity, as shown in the popular *Csardas.* In the slow, horizontal progression section, long gliding steps are taken in a circle and then suddenly are transformed into fast, vertical action in which the men jump and turn with furious agility and strength. This dance is said to be symbolic of the Hungarian's dignity contrasted with his impulsive romanticism.

Hungarian folk dance usually starts on an upbeat with stamps or heel clicks. This preparatory action is always directed down into the earth. There are many abrupt stops, fragmented rhythms, and breaks at the end of phrases. While the steps are relatively simple, they are always performed with great tension and precision. One of the most basic, a two-count step-close, is performed with no observable weight change, the body being held erect and perfectly balanced. A simple variation is the addition of another two-count rise to the toes and lowering to the heels. The men click their heels once, twice, or more times on the third count. Another popular variation, in three counts, starts with knee bends and then a step-close which easily develops into a sideward sliding motion.

The step-hop, with leg lifting high and toe pointed down, and the swinging leg slap occur in many dances. There are innumerable breaks to end a phrase or figure. For example, the man steps sideward on the right toe, heel out (ct. 1); left heel raises and turns outward, weight on both toes (ct. 2); heels click together, hold on toes (ct. 3-4). The woman hops on the left foot, pointing the right sideward or forward (ct. 1); leap onto the right, pointing left sideward or forward (ct. 2); click heels and hold on toes (ct. 3-4).

**37**

For which of these steps: bleking, mazurka, polka, schottische, two-step, varsouvienne, is the first line of notes appropriate accompaniment? the second line? Can you draw the foot pattern of each step to correspond to the notes?

Evaluation Questions

RHYTHMIC PATTERN

The body is always carried tall and styled as a proud horseman, much like the Polish dancer. There is a strong projection of assurance and exhilaration, each dancer being in complete control of himself.

Unusual variations are introduced by the dance leader who sets the initial action for the others to follow. Partners often stand opposite each other, mirroring each others' action. The men cover great space with broad leaps or swift, small running steps. The woman matches her partner's action but is always shy, dainty, and more restrained. Arms usually move in opposition to the feet, seldom overhead, and are crossed on the chest only when hopping backward.

## IRELAND (CELTIC)

As in so many other countries, the circle is an ancient formation in Ireland. Especially at May Day celebrations, a serpentine is still performed around a tree or bonfire. The dancers always move from right to left; it was only when signs were not propitious in the old days that dances would be performed from left to right. In one ancient field dance, *Rinceadhfada,* three dancers, holding the ends of kerchiefs, led couples in a slow processional; then in faster tempo the couples would pass under the raised kerchiefs of the leaders and would move off in semicircles to form new figures.

Today, there is a sharp division of Irish dance into the group village dances of ancient origins and the competitive small group or solo dances of more recent development.

The village dances, expressive of the wit and vigor of the people, filled with fantasy and superstition, are performed with exuberant emotion.

Diagram C:
RHYTHMIC PATTERN

Usually gay and boisterous they are marked by heavy accents into the earth. Current circle dances, May Dances, and chain processionals, where the dancers are still connected with handkerchiefs, are examples of these.

From the more urban areas come the small group and solo dances. The *Jig*, usually a solo dance, is a staccato clog-shuffle movement; the *Reel*, performed more smoothly, is reminiscent of the sophisticated courts and the control of the church; the *Hornpipe* is a rustic clog dance of sailor ancestry. The Irish today use the same basic steps for the Reel and the Jig.

The solo forms use complicated footwork, beating the feet into the floor, and are improvised from quite rigid patterns. The arms hang passively at the sides and the body is held undeviatingly erect, thus not distracting from the brilliant footwork. The weight is held well back of the central line of the body, and there is a tendency to move backward more than forward.

### ISRAEL

While Israel, created in 1948, is really not a European country, it has absorbed folk dances from Northern, Central, and Southern Europe, and folk dances from Israel are very popular in most schools. There is a blend of ex-patriots, with the traditions and practices of their native lands which include even those from the Orient and the Americas. Surrounded by Middle Eastern influences, Israel is developing a popular folk dance of its own. Many dances are purposefully choreographed and include Yemenite and Debka steps, which are almost always set to ancient Hebrew songs. These dances, with their stress on group unity, love of the new land, and faith in their youth, reflect the nation's struggle for identity and freedom. Here is one exciting evidence of a people deliberately using folk dance to integrate its citizenry and to enhance nationalism.

There is a characteristic dignity and reserve in almost all of the dances, even though there are periods of abandon in some of the figures. Steps are usually taken flat-footed, with knees soft and the feet turned out. Dancers usually stand close to each other in the *Horah* circle dances. Occasionally, dancers drop hands and turn about themselves, but there is a persistent return to the unified circle.

Not all of the dances are circle *Horahs*. There are many couple dances; some are courtship dances, and others are for innumerable celebrations of a social or a political nature. Because the dances are being choreographed today, content tends to derive from current happenings. *Let Us Go To The Desert*, an Israeli army dance, and *Mayim*, a Kibbutz creation based on the joy of having enough water, are examples.

## ITALY (LATIN)

Italy, the cradle of the Renaissance, is famous for its many dancing masters who were responsible for initiating the great European court dances. Perhaps it is because of the great emphasis here that so little reference is made to the actual folk dance. While there is a folk dance in Italy, there has been widespread assimilation of dances from other lands as well.

Generally the village dances are careless in rhythm, noisy and exuberant in feeling. In some there is tense and neat movement with outbursts of pantomime; in almost all, there is clapping, stamping, heel tapping, and whistling. There is universal reliance on literal stories and a kind of acting out of relationships among people. Both pantomime and farce are still popular in this land of their greatest development.

The rather tedious story relating the *Tarantella* dance to the tarantula insect is relevant only in that it establishes the quality of the movement as frenzied, sufficient to induce perspiration, and, finally, exhaustion. It is a gay and animated dance with considerable pantomime, usually concerned with guessing how many fingers can be seen in a suddenly opened hand.

The original Galliard (*Romanesca*), sometimes called Five-Steps (*Cinque-pas*), and the *Saltarello*, a 2/4 couple dance from ancient Rome, are all performed in lively and abandoned style. There is much display of the ladies' charms and the men's cleverness. While the dancers' feet move evenly with the accompaniment, it seems a casual and almost aimless performance.

**40**

## POLAND (SLAVIC)

Poland is one European country that has preserved its folk dance in an active form. In almost all of the dances there is a characteristic accent on the second beat, as in the gallop of a horse. This accent is usually taken as a slide or step, with the other leg thrusting up or out; or the second step may sweep out in a great circle reaching step. If there is a third step, as in 3/4 meter, it serves only as a preparation for the upcoming accent on the second beat.

The back is erect, with shoulders, neck, and head held firm and high, like a regimental horseman. The arms usually swing in opposition to the legs or are held at a 45-degree angle to the body. The men often sweep their arms through a figure-eight pattern as with a whip. The man leads the group figure dances with his left hand pointing the line of progression, his right arm around the lady's waist. Only when the men dance alone are their hands on their hips. In many of these dances the girls place their hands on the upper forearms of their partners, and both sweep their feet in large circles on the second part of full turns. In several of the fast dances, the girls are flung high in the fertility leap, the men springing high into the air and then falling onto one or both knees.

The *Polonaise*, a couple dance of court origin, is performed with gravity and splendor, moving as a proud procession with occasional bows and partner changes. The *Mazur* is a romping circle dance in which the couples seem to turn endlessly. As a popular form, it is called the Mazurka. *Krakowiak*, a circle dance with song accompaniment, is marked by considerable improvisation on basic steps, taken in the center of the circle.

## PORTUGAL (LATIN)

There are many features which the dance of Spain and the Basque country share. The desert plains of Spain and the rugged mountains of the North are replaced by green and fertile soil in Portugal. Sun drenched and having a long seacoast for fishing, the people are more relaxed and easy in their movements. Their dances are gay and free, with little of the pride and restraint of the Spaniard. There is simplicity of rhythm and patterning in most of their dances except for some in the South where Moorish influences have been felt. From Africa and Brazil has come *Fado*, a melancholy dance-song which is especially popular throughout Portugal.

Many current folk dances are in two parts. In the first, while singing the verse, couples walk solemnly around a circle, then during the refrain, perform fast yet simple steps accompanied by finger snaps and hand claps. Couple dances, like *Fandango*, provide for a display of technical skill. The

**41**

first dancer sets the rhythm for endless variations. Some of the fishermen's dances have elusive and strange rhythms for their very simple steps.

As in Spain and Italy, the dances are strongly influenced by the church calendar and are used freely in celebrations. The influence of England is strongly felt in the regular 2/4 and 3/4 metric patterns, the running steps, chassés, smooth polkas, and schottisches. The *pas de basque* and waltz are equally popular.

Almost all of the dances are performed in either couple or small group formations. The bodies are relaxed and easy, arms swinging with the pulse of the body action, fingers snapping to accent the underlying beat. There are fast foot-beats in front and back of the supporting leg, alternating with tiny leaps.

## ROUMANIA (LATIN)

There is great variety to the dances of Roumania because of the numerous invasions, annexations, and immigrations of people from other lands. Similar in many respects to the Slavic and Middle Eastern dance forms there is considerable Gypsy influence in both music and dance.

Of the ancient dances, the chain *Horas* are still popular. These are performed with slow stateliness followed by unusually fast sections, after which the circle dissolves into couples dancing with each other. There is a contrasting somberness and gaity to these dances which tests the agility, endurance, and expressiveness of the performers.

The dancers maintain a proud, erect carriage, covering the ground with small irregularly timed running steps. In their innumerable turns, the partners often assume a waist-hold position and, leaning away from each other, spin rapidly with two steps on the heels or the balls of the feet during each complete turn.

In the higher mountain regions, there are dances similar to those of the Hungarians and Basques. In these, the precise stepping is contrasted with furious leaps and turns, deep knee bends, leg thrusts, and dainty foot beats.

Some of the basic steps include two-steps, walks, runs (especially runs to the side), pivots, stamps, and heel clicks. The rhythms are usually quite complicated and are often dictated to the musicians by the dancers.

## RUSSIA (SLAVIC)

It is almost impossible to clearly differentiate the dance styles found in the fifteen areas that compose the Union of Soviet Socialist Republics. With such vast and different regions, each subject to different as well as common influences, there is the widest possible variation. There are circle

**Evaluation Questions**

**What are some of the characteristics of folk dances of mountainous regions?**

dances, processionals, line dances, couple dances, chains, and, near the Western borders, some figure dances which include polkas and mazurkas.

An interesting differentiation has been indicated between the long, free leaps performed by the horse-riding peoples of the plains and the high, precise leaps of those from the Caucasus mountain region. According to several records, more lyrical movement is found in warmer climates with action of great vigor and range in colder areas.

The old dances have a slow, dignified, and deliberate beginning which contrasts with the rapid, vivacious, and humorous action. While few of the dances ever attain the ferocity of the other Slavic dances, the men are remarkably agile and daring. In one dance the men express their skill and virility to the women, coaxing them to follow. The women glide smoothly after them, covering their faces with their hands and always bending to one side. The men drop onto one knee, twirl, and then leap up to follow their ladies. In one Central Asian dance, the women stabilize their torsos and, with arms high over their heads, sway their heads from side to side while pressing the palms of their hands together.

In some of the courtship or work dances the girls flutter their fingers up and down their arms and necks, pointing to their embroidered sleeves and collars. In some others they mime characteristic work movements and wave the ever-present kerchief. In some harvest dances, the arms are brought up to the chest and then opened gradually in a gesture of giving.

Most of the dances are unstructured and are open for the leader's improvisation and imagination. With the introduction by singers or musicians, the dancers form a ring and begin slowly to move counter-clockwise with smooth, gliding steps. The circle grows larger as more dancers join it. With no warning, one of the men flings himself into the center and begins his solo; this initiates competition among many solo dancers. The tempo increases and the dance finally ends with rapid whirling turns.

A leap or jump accompanies the high notes, and on the low ones the body droops, even into a collapse. It is not clear if these movements are intended to be expressive to the observer or are just the dancer's reaction to the music.

Folk dancing is still performed in the more rural areas of Russia, though the old forms are giving way to new versions. Fortunately, the government is carrying on a program of recording and reforming many of the dances so that the old forms will not entirely disappear. Some contemporary dances are based on such themes as *Dance Of The Great Tractor Driver* and *Dance Of The Gallant Soldier Of The Great Homeland*. As in Scotland and in many Slavic countries, folk dance has come to be a way of identifying units within the army and work force.

## SCANDINAVIA (TEUTONIC)

Almost all of the dances of Denmark, Norway, and Sweden have common movement and rhythmic patterns. The old forms were usually long, accompanied by Viking and Norse songs. Some of the old religious dances honored Thor, and the sacred drinking horns came to be a part of the ritual. It is possible that remnants of Eastern influences still remain in the folk arts of these countries. In the Faroe islands, an ancient chain dance is still performed, accompanied by an old chant. The step-close, twice to the right and once to the left, is repeated over and over, with the arms swinging backward and forward in increasing range. Remnants of the old fertility dances are still performed when the men swing their legs high over their kneeling partners.

DENMARK. In Denmark, there is little flamboyance or emotional contrast but there is considerable spontaneity and clowning. Similar to the dances of Holland and Germany, there are two characteristic dances for men, one a fighting figure and the other called the Mill-Wheel, a relic of sun-worshipping rites.

Steps are usually small with the foot carefully lifted and put down firmly for the turns. For greater impetus, the partners lean away from each other on turns. With little curved movement, there is marked emphasis on the down action. A preliminary stamp is taken in front of the supporting foot.

Basic steps include walks, runs, gallops, skips, and waltzes, the latter being performed by two gliding steps followed by a close. The polkas are usually small, with or without a tiny hop. Sometimes a pivot step is used to travel and, unlike other dancers, the Dane takes the weight on the right foot when travelling to the left, keeping the left foot behind the right heel, reversing for the other direction.

NORWAY. Because Norway and Denmark were one nation from the early 1300's to the early 1800's, little difference is evidenced in most of the folk dances found today. Remnants of ancient dances, with Norse songs about knights and their ladies, folk spirits and magic, are still found in parts of the high mountain country. These songs and dances were apparently improvised and had complicated rhythms. Some of them were in chain formation, similar to those of the Faroe islands.

The more recent dances are vigorous, free, and more spontaneous than the Danish or Swedish forms. There are remarkable displays of strength, endurance, and agility by the men, with mimicking of fighting and swordplay. The dance for men, called *Halling*, is such a display of difficult leaps, complicated kicks, deep knee bends, and competitive tricks. Some of the arm movements are similar to the actions of a swordsman and warrior.

One of the most characteristic features of Norwegian folk dance is the practice of starting any dance with a stamp on the last bar of the preceding phrase.

SWEDEN. Similar to the rest of the Scandinavian forms, Swedish dances are sober and dignified, marked by the proud and discreet bearing of the performers. Of all the dancers of the North, the Swedish dancers move the most as restrained conquerors do. Partners stand far apart in their dance positions, and their feet remain close to the floor at all times. Aside from an insignificant sway from side to side, there is little movement. The head and shoulders are stiffly erect, and there is only an occasional mild hand clap or stamp at the beginning or the end of a phrase.

One of the best known of the Swedish couple dances, the *Hambo*, with its irregular step pattern, one for the man and another for the woman, is unique in folk dance description. This is one of their dances that travels with greater abandon, especially as the woman soars into the air on the lift.

## SCOTLAND (CELTIC)

Among the Scots there is an almost unbroken line of dance from the earliest Celtic ancestors. The continuing link of forms to the soldiers, maintained even today by the Highland Regiments, has fostered a deep regard for folk dance. Village dances lost much of their pagan character with the coming of Christianity, and there was an obvious influence from foreign dancing masters.

The true national dance of Scotland is the *Reel*, called the Foursome Reel with two couples, and the Sixsome Reel with three. This is a smooth, gliding dance with much rising and lowering from toes to heels, according to the expression of the music. There are Reels for weddings, holidays, harvests, and victories; indeed, there is a Reel for almost every situation.

Some field dances, ring, chain, and May Day forms, are still popular, but it is the Sword Dance and the Fling that arouse the Scots to national pride today. For the sword dancers, there are many associations with the struggle for freedom. Great competitions of dancers and pipers are common both in the army and among the general population.

The *Fling* and the *Sword* dances are sometimes performed in squares of four or eight dancers, sometimes as a solo. In the early days, if any part of the crossed swords, or even the scabbord, were touched it was an evil omen and was often grounds for imprisonment or death.

The *Fling* is a dance of victory or rejoicing and is performed with a rigid back, straight knees, and a crisp and rapid beating of the legs and feet. Both the Fling and the Sword dance capitalize on neat and feather-like footwork, with a delicate but firm balance of the body over the supporting leg below. Any downward action serves only as a basis for springing up. The weight is carried forward over the toes, and the legs are strong and firm. Unlike the Irish who concentrate their foot action into the ground, the Scots beat their feet in the air. The arms are usually raised overhead but are never closed. Similar to the posture of fencing and the classical ballet, these dances obviously came from the same source.

While some of the dances maintain the old form of a slow section followed by a fast one, this emotionally charged contrast is losing its popularity. The balanced and gay quality of the Sword, the Fling, and the Reel are current favorites.

## SPAIN (LATIN)

In the Basque region of Northern Spain and in some of the more rural areas, chain or circle dances are still performed which are similar to those of Greece and the Middle East. Almost every province has some kind of a *Jota*, rooted in the soil of the area, and which is still performed at festive occasions in the village square and in front of the church after Mass. Many of these old forms have been forsaken, however, and the more spectacular Iberian Classical Dance has become increasingly popular, though hardly ever involving all the people. Among these are the classic forms with their formal and dignified patterns, and the Gypsy *Flamenco* with its arrogant, improvisational forms. More than ever, these two are overlapping though they do retain distinctive characteristics.

The classical form, learned by all well-born Spanish girls, is identified mainly as the *Seguidillas*. This form is set with three or more stanzas (*coplas*), repeated musically, but performed with varied steps. The body is held high, with head erect, throat curved. The action is formal, majestic, and supple. There are abrupt starts and stops, with castanet sounds important to its style. The *Flamenco* form, developed by the Gypsies from the cave region of South Spain, has a free expression in which the dancer dictates his own rhythm and movement pattern. There is much improvisation and display of virtuosity, with unexpected bursts of enthusiasm and melancholy. The spine is rigid, and carriage of the head and shoulders is arrogant. The tossing head, anguished trembling, and sultry expression, all marked by startling starts and stops, are ever present. The fingernail snap, finger snap, hand clap, and occasional castanet playing involve complex rhythms that often differ from those of the heel beats.

The rustic Spanish folk dance, however, while using heel beats and hand claps, has none of the rigid style of the *Flamenco* or Classical dance. A rural *Jota* is usually broad and sweeping, with castanets held at arms length; there are fast foot beats, both in the air and on the ground. There are many fast turns, crescendos and abrupt stops. These seem to reflect a simple and happy people, quite unlike the moody Gypsy. In *Old Danza*, the arms and body are held immobile and only the feet glide around the path of the circle.

In almost all of the existing forms, there is an obvious Moorish influence, with complicated, broken rhythms. In part, this may be due to the Gypsy musicians who travelled through Spain as the only available sources for accompaniment, thus probably imposing many of their own rhythms on the dances of many areas.

## YUGOSLAVIA (SLAVIC)

Of all the dance forms, the *Kolo* is the most pervasive in this land which consists of Serbia, Croatia, Montenegro, Herzegovina, Macedonia, Bosnia, and Slovenia. There is obvious influence from Greece, Turkey, and Italy in the central and southern part of the country and from Austria and Hungary in the North. In rural areas, there are remnants of old fertility rites in a *Kolo* led by a young girl carrying a snake or garland in her hands or draped about her neck.

Almost all of the dances are closed circles, though they sometimes open into a chain. Some are *Kolos* for men or for women, sometimes for both; some may be for young men, for young women, and even for members of a village selected in order of their status. The circle may progress clockwise or counter-clockwise; it may move into the center of the circle and may occasionally break the circle for turns or individual action.

**Hazard a guess as to why the most ancient and most prevalent of the folk dance formations is a circle.**

Evaluation Questions

There are shaking *Kolos* in which small jumps literally shake the dancers, stepping *Kolos* which progress close to the ground with an accompanying trembling of the dancers, and hopping *Kolos* made up of repeated step-close and step-hop patterns.

Dancers move in accord with the rhythm set by the words of accompanying songs, though the leader sometimes marks his own rhythm and tempo and even improvises his steps. The leader not only guides but inspires both dancers and musicians. When he tires, he passes his responsibility by passing his handkerchief to someone else. No matter how complex the superimposed rhythm of the accompaniment, the dancers maintain a steady underlying beat.

Dancers linked in circles hold fingers, hands, elbows, shoulders, waists, or belts. At the start there is an electrifying tension, and then there is a release into an undulating, wave-like motion evidenced both in bodies and in encircling arms. These undulations are said to be like the sweeping motion of the earth and the celestial bodies.

There is a curious relaxed knee action with a strong drive through the heel and into the earth, rising again to drive down once more. Sometimes the circling stops and the dancers rise and fall on the supporting toes, then drop low before continuing.

In some *Kolos* the dancers step to the side and close sharply, step again to the side and then add some extraneous movement such as a leg swing, body dip, shoulder shake, or head roll. In one of the young men's *Kolos*, the performers carry swords, sweeping them in great circles as they leap and twist about in the center of the group.

When the women dance they are almost always modest and reserved, their eyes lowered to the earth. In some of the Moslem areas where women are not free to leave the house, they perform *Kolos* within the harems. In Croatia, however, the women circle about with bodies trembling, heads flung back, gaze open and out as the bodies strain backward in an arc. There is no loss of conscious awareness of the group in spite of the hypnotic appearance of the dancers.

Regardless of church or political influence, the *Kolos* continue throughout the land, though in the remote mountain areas they have changed less from their early form. In the North there have been widespread changes, influenced by dances from Austria and Hungary. In this area, waltzes, polkas, hand claps, foot stamps, and swinging arms have become a part of their folk dance.

# 6

# Aids for the
# Student Dancer

For sheer fun, nothing can surpass learning more and more folk dances. There is a unique excitement in this kind of movement. While there are some dances for women alone, the great majority are for both men and women, boys and girls. Unfortunately, folk dance will lose much of its vitality, as well as its reason for being, if it is performed only by girls. Every effort should be made to have this experience coeducational.

As a person learns more of the reasons for doing these dances, a new enjoyment develops. And as skills increase, folk dance becomes even more exciting. In addition to learning to do the dance comes the personal challenge to move with greater control and coordination which are necessary to attain style.

Any activity that differs from one that has been done before demands special attention to new abilities and to the development of sensitivity. The best performance in folk dance requires balance, coordination, and control.

One of the greatest problems of the beginning folk dancer is learning to use as little effort as is necessary, a requirement for the greatest effectiveness. Consideration of the simple principles of body mechanics will be helpful. The following exercises are suggested not so much to help you do more complicated folk dance steps but to help you understand how to control your body in relation to the stresses of gravity. Are the principles of balanced body parts and stable base clear? Certainly, successful action demands such control.

## FOR INCREASED BALANCE AND BODY ALIGNMENT

From a centered standing position, feet easy and about 3-4 inches apart.

**50**

1. Concentrate on a vertical line from midway between the balls of the feet up through the center of the hips, back, neck, and head. Look into a mirror and check. Don't collapse; hold the position and breathe easily.

2. Now, turn your attention to a side view. Grip with your buttocks and tuck your hips under your torso. This should help to put the parts where they belong. Gripping with the buttocks will also straighten knock knees if you have them. Notice how your shoulders and head readjust. Pull up with the back of your neck and balance your chin parallel to the sky. You can still turn your head! Don't collapse, hold it and breathe easily. Check up on your vertical line again.

3. Drop forward from the waist and shake the tension from your arms and back. Come up to erect standing and repeat the techniques of Number 2 above. Check both front and side views in the mirror.

4. Stand as far away from the mirror as possible; check your standing position from both front and side, and then walk forward toward the mirror. What do you see? Do you keep the vertical line or

   a. Does your head jut forward like a turtle?
   b. Do your hips push back and make a shelf?
   c. Do you strain back against your knees?
   d. Are you walking from your knees instead of from your hips?
   e. Are your arms clutched to your sides as if they would fly off?
   f. Do you bounce toward the ceiling as you step forward?
   g. Do your feet track diagonally East and West instead of forward?
   h. Does one foot perform a fancy flip, the other a lazy drag?

   If any of these things happens in a simple walk, think how the error will be exaggerated in dancing!

   A functional walk starts with a vertical body line, legs swinging forward from the hips, with force applied through the center of the body *in line with the direction* you are going. The weight moves onto the heel and through a foot placed straight ahead.

5. Go back to the standing position and concentrate on the vertical line buttock-grip technique. Sway forward and back on your feet until you find that point at which your weight seems centered over the base below.

   Now imagine a rope hanging from the ceiling, directly over your head; hook the lower end of the rope to the crown of your head and imagine the rope pulling up. Grip with the buttocks, and pretend you have a very heavy tail hanging straight down toward the floor. The tail must not curl up over your back nor must it be pulled in between your legs. Let the arms hang easily, let the tail hang easily! Sway forward and back again until you find a centered position over your base. *Hang on to that center.*

6. Now do the same thing with the feet close together.
7. Now do the same thing from a tip-toe position. If you grip with your heels as well as with your buttocks, your control will be easier.

## FOR IMPROVED LEG AND ANKLE COORDINATION

1. Standing with feet parallel and slightly apart:

   a. Slowly change weight from one foot to the other, rising up to the half toe, lifting heel, flexing knee.
   b. Same thing, letting the toes barely leave the floor, and twice as fast.
   c. Develop into a running prance, being sure that the push-off comes through the entire foot, finishing with the toe last. Feel as if you were pushing the floor down or as a diver pushes the diving board *down* in order to get a lift *up*.
   d. Do each of these in an 8-count phrase. Complete the three sets with a change-change-hold, finishing with last foot up.
   a. Try to concentrate on the centered position, with all body parts in correct alignment. Be precise in position, rhythm, and tempo. Do the same 8-count phrase patterns moving through space. Try the same series, changing direction at the end of each 8-count phrase.

2. Perform the prance in your own circle on the floor, accenting the (1) of a 3/4 and the (1) of a 4/4 rhythmic pattern. Try accenting with a heavier step and then adding a clap. Be sure to use the *full ankle action* and *push-off* with the toes. When you land, reverse this action by coming down through the ball of the foot and into the heel as the knee bends. Keep your knee over the big toe.

3. Minimize the prance into a little run, using small steps. Keep the ankle action and be sure you push off with the toes. Try accenting the (1) of a 3/4 and the (1) of a 4/4 meter as you did in the prance. Check on the vertical body alignment. Don't collapse!

4. Try the same little run in one place, then start turning to the right and then to the left, finally just running in place again.

5. Extend the little run so that you travel through space; try to turn yourself around as you progress. Do it in both directions. Remember to *hang on* to your center and to keep your vertical alignment. Don't try to complete a whole circle each time; leave this for later when you are more sure of your balance. When you turn, you are very apt to get dizzy. In addition to feeling the extended vertical line and hanging on to your center, it is best not to let your gaze wander through space.

Evaluation Questions

**How can you improve leg and ankle coordination for performing folk dance?**

Try to find a stable point in line with where you are going, and let your gaze return firmly to this point after every turn. This is called "spotting" and is used by tumblers and dancers alike. If you do get dizzy, stop and lower your head and shoulders for a moment or turn in the other direction to unwind! No matter how awkward you may feel, you will be surprised how quickly you will accommodate to turning if you will only practice.

## FOR RHYTHMIC PERCEPTION AND PERFORMANCE

No matter how well controlled the movement, it is of little use if it fails to progress and arrive at the right time. Becoming sensitive to rhythm and time relationships and developing the ability to move in relation to them is very important. The following exercises certainly will be helpful.

1. Listen to music with a strong definition of underlying beat in 2/4, 3/4, 4/4, 6/8, and 7/8 meters. Try to identify the primary accent, regardless of melodic decoration of the underlying beat.

   For 2/4 meter, note the recurrent accent on (1) of 2 cts.
   *1* 2; *1* 2; *1* 2; *1* 2; *1* 2; *1* 2

   For 3/4 meter, note the recurrent accent on (1) of 3 cts.
   *1* 2 3; *1* 2 3; *1* 2 3; *1* 2 3; *1* 2 3

   For 4/4 meter, note the recurrent accent on (1) of 4 cts.
   *1* 2 3 4; *1* 2 3 4; *1* 2 3 4; *1* 2 3 4

   For 6/8 meter, note the recurrent accent on (1) of 6 cts.
   *1* 2 3 4 5 6; *1* 2 3 4 5 6; *1* 2 3 4 5 6;

For 7/8 meter, note the recurrent accent on (1) of 7 cts.
*1* 2 3 4 5 6 7; *1* 2 3 4 5 6 7

2. After you are certain that you can recognize this recurrent accent, clap to coincide with it. Accent the (1) of each measure.

3. When you can both hear and clap with the accent, walk on each beat, stepping with a heavier step; later add a hand clap on each accent.

4. Without any clue to the music or meter, respond to a variety of rhythms. If a pianist is available, ask him to play the same melody in different meters. See if you can still identify the underlying beat.

5. Listen to simple waltz music (3/4 meter) and try to clap the (1) accent of a *four-beat* measure. Is it clear that this does *not* fit? Reverse this, listening to 4/4 music as you attempt to clap three beats to the measure. This should help you to find the more comfortable and obvious pattern.

6. Listen to strongly accented 6/8 music. Note the phrases of 4, 6, or 8 sets of 6/8 measures. Stop the music after 3, 5, or 7 measures and notice how incomplete it seems. The ability to recognize larger and smaller phrases will be helpful. Some folk dance music is not written in 2-4-8-16 measure phrases and will present a problem. Most of such accompaniment is in even length phrases.

7. Walk slowly in a circle, with one step on each beat of a 4/4 meter. Try this *without* music, providing your own sound accompaniment, such as dum de dum de. Keep these units as even as inches on a ruler.
   1   2   3   4

   Next, double each step and accompany with:
   dum   dum   de   de   dum   dum   de   de.
   1     &    2    &    3     &    4    &

   Next triple each step and accompany with:
   dum   dum   dum   de   de   de   dum   dum   dum   de   de   de.
   1     &     a    2    &    a    3     &     a    4    &    a

   It may be easier to take the four-count walk on each side of a square; then you will have a shape and direction difference to remind you of the change. In this case, repeat each pattern four times before increasing the action.

8. With other members of your group, sit on the floor in a circle. One person starts clapping a simple rhythmic pattern, for example, a 3/4 pattern accenting the first beat of each measure. When tempo and

**Evaluation Questions**

How can you improve your rhythmic perception and performance in folk dancing?

accent are clear, everyone in the circle should clap the same pattern. Change leaders, rhythm, and tempo.

9. Walk in a circle, step on the first beat and clap on the second of a 4/4 pattern. Reverse this by clapping on the first beat and stepping on the second. Try to alternate these without losing track of the underlying beat.

10. With a group sitting on the floor in a circle, have someone establish a simple rhythmic pattern in a clearly defined tempo. Each individual then takes his turn clapping one or two measures of the established pattern. Try to keep the tempo clear and don't lose your turn. When the tempo wavers, it will be evident. Try to maintain a consistent underlying beat. Most people will be more sensitive if they keep a foot, head, shoulder, or some part of their body moving in order to maintain the pulse.

## CLUES TO LEADERS

Leadership in folk dance occurs in a variety of ways. Sometimes it is evidenced in a single figure leading a line or chain of dancers; or it may come from a musician or a caller. In the couple dances, however, leadership is almost always the role of the man who both sets and maintains the action.

Prerequisite to good leadership is the assurance which comes from knowledge of the step, the pattern, and the style. This is of no avail if the leader fails to take the initiative. He must be firm and thereby will reassure his partner and other dancers, both psychologically and physically. The inclination of the body, suitably sized steps, and a firm hold will all

**55**

be helpful. It is the duty of the leader to anticipate future patterns and to make sure that both he and his partner or group negotiate transitions in order to be ready for action to come. Actually, this is a rehearsal of those characteristics of support, reliability, firm decision, and gentle persuasion implicit in the traditional role of the man.

One simple technique for identifying and practicing this role for couple dances is to stand opposite the partner, holding both of his hands in yours. This role is even easier if tried in the traditional social dance position so that the hand at the girl's back can indicate turn directions; greater pressure for her movement forward, less for movement backward.

Another helpful technique is to keep the same closed dance position and practice leading first with one hand, the other dropped to the side, then reversing, with the other hand holding. When the regular position is again assumed and both hands are available for guidance, it will be obvious how helpful this is. Practice and a little assurance will result in some degree of leadership ability.

Of course, leading is particularly difficult if the partner resists and is confusing as well if both attempt to lead.

## CLUES FOR THE FOLLOWER

Perhaps the greatest attribute of a good follower is the psychological and literal acceptance of the leader's capacity to lead. The follower should be sensitive, relaxed, and *ready* to be led. Any excessive tension or determination to follow her own inclination will lead to disaster for the couple.

The girl should be balanced and ready to move, capable of maintaining her own erect posture without physically leaning on her partner. This takes as much effort and consideration as a lively conversation, with no rude interruptions from either. As the pattern for leading is symbolic of man's traditional role, so is following that of the woman. The receptivity to man's leadership, sensitvity to and acceptance of his guidance, reliance on his judgment, and value for his concern are all inherent in this role.

Regardless of the girl's skill, rhythmic sensitivity, or personal conviction, she must follow the leader's direction even though she is sure he is in error. In cases where girls assume men's parts, they should understand that they are taking an unnatural role, as far as folk dance is concerned.

## CLUES FOR GROUP INTERACTION

The only way to develop a feeling of group unity is to practice group unity. But first you must understand the action for yourself. Not only is skill in performing the steps necessary, but you must understand when each movement occurs and where it goes. After these factors are clear, the interaction of the dancers can be rehearsed. As soon as dancers begin to feel the group pulsations, sweeps, and tensions, then the magic of real folk dance has started.

One good way to begin to feel this kind of interaction is to perform a simple circular figure together. Standing close in a ring, clasp hands and begin an easy knee bounce with everyone moving up and down at the same time. Let the body, arms, and head relax to blend into a subtle pulsation. Slowly begin to move in either direction with a series of small step-close steps to the side. Repeat the standing pulsation and then the step-close again; vary the size and direction of these steps, moving in and out of the circle. Everyone should learn to *feel* himself as a part of the group. Let one dancer break the circle and lead the rest in spirals, lines, and serpentines, returning again to the standing pulsation.

Because this simple figure is similar to many of the circle dances, it might be appropriate to start with a Yugoslavian *Horo* or with an Israeli *Horah,* with the exciting music of the country. When the group seems to move as one, each dancer adjusting his individual action to that of the others, fitting pace and accent, then some coordinated effort and group interaction will be both seen and felt.

## SIMPLE ETIQUETTE FOR DANCERS

Because folk dancing is a vigorous activity, it is advisable to dress in loose, comfortable clothes. Girls should wear full skirts and flats; boys should be dressed in clean shirts and trousers or shorts. Frequent bathing and use of deodorants will be appreciated by all participants.

There are no universal patterns of behavior and manners but general procedures for civil interaction of people should be observed. When a teacher or group leader is explaining or demonstrating, it is to your advantage to be quiet and listen.

In couple dances where the boy assumes the role of leader, he should make every effort to understand and practice his responsibility. The girl, in this case, should follow quietly and pleasantly. In all of these relationships, a simple kindness and regard for all concerned should prevail. It is possible to use a group situation like this as a laboratory for the practice of social amenities such as introductions, simple manners, and social behavior. The usual social dance customs of our country are observed though it is not necessarily so in the land of a folk dance's origin. For example, here, the men are expected to escort ladies from the performance area while elsewhere it sometimes is customary to leave them standing alone.

## KEEPING A RECORD OF DANCES YOU KNOW

Unless you frequently review the dances you have learned, you are apt to forget the formation, sequence of steps, patterns, or appropriate music. One way to retain this information is to develop a file with such relevant material recorded on cards. While you may have to return to the original source at times, this constitutes an easy and quick reference. The example here is only one of many ways to accomplish this.

Side One

DANCE: <u>Horah</u>                                 Source: Cochem, C.,

COUNTRY: Israel                                <u>Jewish Holiday Dances</u>

FORMATION: Dancers in a closed circle, hands on shoulders of dancers
on either side.

STEPS: Three steps to right, kick left, step left and hop, kick right.

CUES: Step, step, step, kick, step, kick.

MUSIC: Hava Nagilla (Folkcraft F1110-B)

Side Two

STYLE: Starts slowly to establish rhythm and unity of group. Steps are
smooth and pulsating. As tempo increases, so does intensity
and excitement of the dancers. Never lose control, never
break the circle. If the original circle is too large, form a
smaller one on the inside. These circles move both clockwise
and counter-clockwise.

# Selected References

There are many books, pamphlets, and manuals readily available which describe folk dances. Some are collections from several countries; others include dances from only one country. Here are a few that will be useful.

## FOLK DANCES

ALFORD, VIOLET, (ed.). Handbooks of European National Dance: *Dances of Austria* (Breuer, 1948); *Dances of Bulgaria* (Katsarvous, n. d.); *Dances of Czechoslovakia* (Lubinova, 1949); *Dances of Denmark* (Jeppesen, 1951); *Dances of England and Wales* (Karpeles and Blake, 1951); *Dances of Finland* (Heikel and Collan, 1948); *Dances of France I: Brittany and Bourbonnais* (Dubois and Andral, 1950); *Dances of France II: Provence and Alsace* (Tennevin and Texier, 1951); *Dances of Germany* (Fyte, 1951); *Dances of Greece* (Crosfield, 1948); *Dances of Hungary* (Buday, 1950); *Dances of Italy* (Galanti, 1950); *Dances of Netherlands* (van der Ven-Ten Bensel, 1949); *Dances of Norway* (Semb, 1951); *Dances of Portugal* (Armstrong, 1948); *Dances of Scotland* (Milligan and MacLennan, 1951); *Dances of Spain I: South, Centre, and Northwest* (Armstrong, 1950); *Dances of Spain II: Northeast and East* (Armstrong, 1951); *Dances of Sweden* (Salven, 1949); and *Dances of Switzerland* (Witzig, 1949). New York: Chanticleer Press, 1948-51. (Published under the auspices of The Royal Academy of Dancing and the Ling Physical Education Association.)

ANDERSON, ELLIE and J. M. DUTHIE, *A Complete Guide to Scottish Country Dancing*, Edinburgh: McDougall's Educational Company,

BELIAJUS, FINADAR V., *Dance and Be Merry*, Vol. I, Chicago: Clayton F. Summy, 1940.

———, *Dance and Be Merry*, Vol. II, Chicago: Clayton F. Summy, 1942.

———, *Dances of Latvia*, Chicago: Clayton F. Summy, 1952.

BURCHENAL, ELIZABETH, *Dances of the People*, New York: G. Schirmer, Inc., 1913.

———, *Folk Dances of Denmark*, New York: G. Schirmer, Inc., 1915.

# SELECTED REFERENCES

——, *Folk Dances of Finland,* New York: G. Schirmer, Inc., 1915.

——, *Folk Dances from Old Homelands,* New York: G. Schirmer, Inc., 1922.

——, *Merrily Dance,* Delaware, Ohio: Cooperative Recreation Service, 1947.

——, *Folk Dances of Germany,* New York: G. Schirmer, Inc., 1938.

——, *Folk Dances and Singing Games,* New York: G. Schirmer, Inc., 1933.

——, *National Dances of Ireland,* New York: A. S. Barnes & Co., Inc., 1925.

BERGQUIST, NILS, *Swedish Folk Dances,* New York: A. S. Barnes, 1914.

BOVBJERG, VIGGO, *Danish Folk Dances,* Chicago: H. T. FitzSimmons, 1917.

BERGMAN, MARION, *The Russian-American Dance Book,* New York: A. S. Barnes & Co., Inc., 1947.

BRYANS, HELEN and JOHN MADSEN, *Scandinavian Dances,* Books I and II, Toronto: Clark, Irwin and Company, Ltd., 1942.

COCHEM, CORRINE, *Palestine Dances,* New York: Behrman House, 1946.

——, *Jewish Holiday Dances,* New York: Behrman House, 1948.

CZARNOWSKI, LUCILLE, *Folk Dance Teaching Clues,* Palo Alto: The National Press, 1963.

DUGGAN, ANNE SCHLEY, *The Folk Dance Library,* New York: A. S. Barnes & Co., Inc., 1948. Five volumes: *The Teaching of Folk Dance, Folk Dances of European Countries, Folk Dances of the United States and Mexico, Folk Dances of the British Isles,* and *Folk Dances of Scandinavia.*

DUNSING, PAUL, *Dance Lightly,* Delaware, Ohio: Cooperative Recreation Service, 1946.

FLETT, J. F. and T. M., *Traditional Dancing in Scotland,* Nashville: Vanderbilt University Press, 1966.

*Folk Dances Near and Far,* Vols. I-X, San Francisco: Folk Dance Federation of California, Vol. I, 1945; Vol. II, 1946; Vol. III, 1947; Vol. IV, 1948; Vol. V, 1949, Vol. A1 (Beginners), 1960; Vol. B1 (Intermediate), 1950; Vol. C1 (Advanced), 1960; and Vol. A2 (Beginners), 1962.

FOX, G. L. and K. G. MERRILL, *Folk Dancing,* 2nd ed., New York: The Ronald Press Company, 1957.

GATES, EDITH M., *Old Dances from New Nations,* Chicago: Clayton F. Summy, 1932.

GEARY, MARJORIE C., *Folk Dances of Czechoslovakia,* New York: A. S. Barnes & Co., Inc., 1922.

GRINDEA, MIRON and CAROLA, *Dances of Roumania,* New York: Crown Publishers, Inc., 1952.

HALL, J. TILLMAN, *Dance,* Belmont, Calif.: Wadsworth Publishing Co., Inc., 1964.

HERMAN, MICHAEL, *Folk Dances for All,* New York: Barnes and Noble, Inc., 1947.

*Highland Dancing,* London: Scottish Official Board of Highland Dancing, 1968. (Available from N. Y. Dance Mart.)

HOLDEN, RICKEY, *Greek Folk Dances,* Newark, N. J.: Folkcraft Press, 1965.

JENSEN, M. B. and C. R., *Beginning Folk Dancing,* New York: Wadsworth Publishing Co., Inc., 1966.

JANKOVIC, LYUBICA and DANICA, *Dances of Yugoslavia,* New York: Crown Publishers, Inc., 1952.

JOUKOWSKY, ANATOL M., *The Teaching of Ethnic Dance,* New York: J. Lowell Pratt and Company, 1965.

KENNEDY, DOUGLAS, *England's Dances, Folk Dancing Today and Yesterday*, London: G. Bell and Sons, Ltd., 1950.

KRAUS, RICHARD, *Folk Dancing: A Guide for Schools, Colleges and Recreation Groups*, New York: The Macmillan Company, 1962.

———, *A Pocket Guide of Folk, Square Dances and Singing Games*, Englewood Cliffs, N. J.: Prentice-Hall, Inc., 1966.

LAGER, HERBERT, *Our Austrian Dances*, Millbrae, Calif.: The National Press, 1952.

LIDSTER, MIRIAM D., and DOROTHY H. TAMBURINI, *Folk Dance Progressions*, New York: Wadsworth Publishing Co., Inc., 1965.

LINDELOF, E. (tr.), *A Collection of Old Swedish Folk Dances*, London: Curwen and Sons, Inc., 1914.

MACLENNAN, D. B., *Highland and Traditional Scottish Dances*, Edinburgh: W. T. McDougall and Company, 1950.

MELLOR, HUGH, *Welsh Folk Dances*, London: Novello and Company, 1935.

O'KEEFE, J. G. and ART O'BRIEN, *A Handbook of Irish Dances*, Dublin: M. H. Gill and Company, 1944.

O'RAFFERTY, PEADAR and GERALD, *Dances of Ireland*, London: Max Parrish and Company, 1953.

PINON, ROGER and HENRI JAMAR, *Dances of Belgium*, London: Max Parrish and Company, 1953.

PETRIDES, THEODIRE and ELFEIDA, *Folk Dances of the Greeks*, New York: Exposition Press, 1961.

REARICK, E. C., *Dances of the Hungarians*, New York: Columbia University Press, 1939.

RICE, CYRIL, *Dancing in Spain*, London: British-Continental Press, 1931.

ROHRBOUGH, LYNN, *Treasures from Abroad*, Delaware, Ohio: Cooperative Recreation Service (Recreation Kit 0), 1942.

SHAMBAUGH, MARY EFFIE, *Folk Dances for Boys and Girls*, New York: A. S. Barnes & Co., Inc., 1929.

———, *Folk Festivals*, New York: A. S. Barnes & Co., Inc., 1929.

SCOTTISH COUNTRY DANCE SOCIETY, *Scottish County Dance Book*, Vols. I-VI, Glasgow: Peterson's Publications, Ltd., 1930. (Available N. Y., C. Fisher.)

SHARP, CECIL J., *An Introduction to English Country Dance*, London: Novello and Company, n. d. (In New York, H. W. Gray.)

———, *The Country Dance Book*, Vols. I-V, London: Novello and Company, 1909-1927. (In New York, H. W. Gray.)

———, *The Morris Books*, Vols. I-V, London: Novello, 1911-1919. (In New York, H. W. Gray.)

———, *The Sword Dances of Northern England*, Vols. I-III, London: Novello and Company, 1912-1913. (In New York, H. W. Gray.)

SPACEK, ANNA and NEVA BOYD, *Folk Dances of Bohemia and Moravia*, Chicago: H. T. FitzSimmons, 1917.

SHAW, LLOYD, *The Round Dance Book*, Caldwell, Idaho: The Caxton Printers, Ltd., 1948.

*Treasure Chest of Dances, Old and New*, New York: Treasure Chest Publications, 1937.

VISKI D., *Hungarian Dances*, London: Simpkin Marshall, Ltd., 1937.

## SELECTED REFERENCES

WAKEFIELD, ELEANOR E., *Folk Dancing in America,* New York: J. Lowell Pratt and Company, 1966.

WOLSKA, HELEN, *Dances of Poland,* London: Max Parrish and Company, 1952.

## ON HISTORY, STYLE, COSTUME

BECK, H. P. (ed.), *Folklore in Action,* Austin: University of Texas Press, 1962.

DOLMETSCH, MABEL, *Dances of Spain and Italy from 1400 to 1600,* London: Routledge and Kegan Paul, 1959.

———, *Dances of England and France from 1450-1600,* London: Routledge and Kegan Paul, 1949.

EVANS, M., *Costumes Throughout the Ages,* Philadelphia: J. B. Lippincott Company, 1930.

*Folkways Records,* 165 West 46th Street, New York, N. Y. 10036: Folk Dance Series.

*Folk Dance Costumes of Europe* (S.P-12) Rhythms Productions, Cheviot Corp., Department M671, Box 34485, Los Angeles, Calif. 90034.

GROVE, LILLY et al., *Dancing,* London: Longmans, Green and Company, 1895. (Part of a series in Badminton Library of Sports and Pastimes.)

HAIRE, FRANCES, *The Folk Costume Book,* New York: A. S. Barnes & Co., Inc., 1934.

HARRISON, JANE E., *The Mythology of All Races,* 13 vols., Boston: Jones, 1931.

HAYES, ELIZABETH, *An Introduction to the Teaching of Dance,* New York: The Ronald Press Company, 1964.

KIMMINS, GRACE T., *The Guild of Play Book of Festival and Dance,* Part III, London: Kurwen and Sons, 1907.

LAWSON, JOAN, *European Folk Dance, Its National and Musical Characteristics,* London: Sir Isaac Pitman & Sons, Ltd., 1953.

LEACH, MARIA (ed.), *Standard Dictionary of Folklore, Mythology, and Legend,* Vols. I-II, New York: Funk and Wagnalls Company, Inc., 1950.

MAGRIEL, PAUL, *A Bibliography of Dancing,* New York: The H. W. Wilson Company, 1936. (See Part III, "Folk, National, Regional, and Ethnological Dances." Yearly supplements to update materials.)

MANN, KATHLEEN, *Peasant Costume in Europe,* New York: The Macmillan Company, 1950.

SPICER, DOROTHY G., *Folk Festivals and the Foreign Community,* New York: The Woman's Press, 1923.

———, *Festivals of Western Europe,* New York: H. W. Wilson Company, 1956.

TILKE, MAX, *Costume Patterns and Designs*: A Survey of Costume Patterns and Designs of All Periods and Nations, New York: Frederick A. Praeger, Inc., 1957.

WILCOX, R. TURNER, *Folk and Festival Costume of the World,* New York: Charles Scribner's Sons, 1965.

# Index